SHARE ABLES

STORIES FROM JESUS

by Dr. Randy T. Johnson

with contributions by:

Chris Cain
John Carter
James Clouse
Trevor Cole
Caleb Combs
Jayson Combs
Josh Combs
Laura Combs
Sierra Combs
Brett Eberle
Eric Jeffrey
Chuck Lindsey
Oralia Lindsey
Wes McCullough
Mark O'Connor
Ken Perry
Holly Wells

Copyright © 2017 The River Church

All rights reserved. No part of this book may be reproduced or transmitted in any form or by any means, electronic or mechanical, including photocopying, recording or by any information storage and retrieval system, without the written permission of The River Church. Inquiries should be sent to the publisher.

First Edition, April 2017

Published by:
The River Church
8393 E. Holly Rd.
Holly, MI 48442

Scriptures are taken from the Bible,
English Standard Version (ESV)

THE RIVER CHURCH

Printed in the United States of America

CONTENTS

WEEK 1: THIS LITTLE LIGHT OF MINE
13 Study Guide
19 Devotion 1: The Bus Driver did it
21 Devotion 2: Salty "Graham" Cracker
23 Devotion 3: Good Samaritan
25 Devotion 4: Not Good Enough Samaritan
27 Devotion 5: Light of the World
29 Devotion 6: The God Who Sees Me

WEEK 2: SUCCESS STARTS WITH STRATEGY
33 Study Guide
39 Devotion 1: Hog Haven
41 Devotion 2: Costly Structural Repairs
43 Devotion 3: Count the Cost
47 Devotion 4: Soldier of the King
49 Devotion 5: Jesus Rocks!
51 Devotion 6: God Almighty

WEEK 3: NEW COVENANT
55 Study Guide
67 Devotion 1: Liberal or Legalist
69 Devotion 2: License to Sin
71 Devotion 3: Sultan of Swat
73 Devotion 4: Crawl like a Camel
75 Devotion 5: Lamb of God
77 Devotion 6: YHWH

WEEK 4: SOWERS KNEEDED
81 Study Guide
87 Devotion 1: Dirty Hands
89 Devotion 2: Twelve Inches
91 Devotion 3: Mystery Man
93 Devotion 4: Abba, Father
95 Devotion 5: An Offshoot
97 Devotion 6: Trinity

WEEK 5: KINGDOM CHAT
101 Study Guide
107 Devotion 1: Pokemon Go...Into all the World
109 Devotion 2: Beans, Rice, and Jesus Christ
111 Devotion 3: A Journey Back
113 Devotion 4: Where's the Next Dance
115 Devotion 5: He Started Start!
117 Devotion 6: Priest and King

WEEK 6: STANDING SMALL
121 Study Guide
127 Devotion 1: Peanuts
129 Devotion 2: Influencer
131 Devotion 3: Bug Me - Forever!
133 Devotion 4: 212 Degrees
135 Devotion 5: House of Bread
137 Devotion 6: Monovision

WEEK 7: THE THRILL IS IN THE SEARCH
141 Study Guide
145 Devotion 1: Hide-N-Seek
147 Devotion 2: Pick'n Forever
149 Devotion 3: Blank Penny
151 Devotion 4: Lose a Friend?
153 Devotion 5: Redeemer
155 Devotion 6: The Provider

WEEK 8: FORGIVE GOD?
159   Study Guide
165 Devotion 1: Paco
167 Devotion 2: The Goal
169 Devotion 3: Kissing Feet
171 Devotion 4: Terrific Testimony
173 Devotion 5: Hack into Hope
175 Devotion 6: Test into Testimony

WEEK 9: BOTTOM OF THE FIRST
179 Study Guide
185 Devotion 1: Cake, Icing, and God
187 Devotion 2: Comfort
189 Devotion 3: Shrewd
191 Devotion 4: Extra Mile
193 Devotion 5: Recharged
195 Devotion 6: Boss

WEEK 10: A-CHORE-ABLE
199 Study Guide
203 Devotion 1: First Love
207 Devotion 2: 180 Degrees
211 Devotion 3: Lost?
213 Devotion 4: Financially Sustain-a-bologna
217 Devotion 5: "Lie" Down in the Arms of Truth
219 Devotion 6: I Am

WEEK 11: TWO SLOTHS
223 Study Guide
229 Devotion 1: Love Me, Love My Son
231 Devotion 2: Rock Your World
233 Devotion 3: Pray Up
235 Devotion 4: God-Made Man
237 Devotion 5: You are Your Father's Son
239 Devotion 6: The Lord of Hosts

WEEK 12: THE INVITATION
243 Study Guide
249 Devotion 1: Wedding Vows
251 Devotion 2: Black Tie Optional
253 Devotion 3: Excuses
255 Devotion 4: Whosoever
257 Devotion 5: Messiah
259 Devotion 6: The Lord our Righteousness

WEEK 13: 1988
263 Study Guide
267 Devotion 1: "Are You Ready?"
269 Devotion 2: Punxsutawney Phil
271 Devotion 3: Do Not Just Look Busy
275 Devotion 4: Pray for Our Children
277 Devotion 5: Strongest Ever
279 Devotion 6: God Everlasting

WEEK 14: GOT OIL?
283   Study Guide
289 Devotion 1: A Walk Down 8 Mile
291 Devotion 2: The Aisle
293 Devotion 3: Eyes Wide Open
295 Devotion 4: "Ready or Not..."
297 Devotion 5: Bridegroom
299 Devotion 6: Got Your Back

WEEK 15: 1 + 0 = 0
303 Study Guide
309 Devotion 1: It's All Chinese to Me
311 Devotion 2: "I Can" Opener
313 Devotion 3: Blame Game
315 Devotion 4: Escar-go-t
319 Devotion 5: Favorite Teacher
321 Devotion 6: 3 Things

WEEK 16: REACH, GATHER, GROW, AND BACK TO REACH
325 Study Guide
329 Testimony 1: Chuck Lindsey
333 Testimony 2: Oralia Lindsey
335 Testimony 3: Josh Combs
339 Testimony 4: Ken Perry
343 Testimony 5: Mark O'Connor
347 Testimony 6: John Carter

WEEK 17: GATHERING WITH THE SAINTS
351 Study Guide
355 Testimony 7: Caleb Combs
359 Testimony 8: Sierra Combs
363 Testimony 9: Trevor Cole
365 Testimony 10: Brett Eberle
367 Testimony 11: Wes McCullough
369 Testimony 12: Eric Jeffrey

WEEK 18: GROWING IN THE WORD
373 Study Guide
377 Testimony 13: Randy "Doc" Johnson
379 Testimony 14: Jayson Combs
381 Testimony 15: Laura Combs
383 Testimony 16: Chris Cain
385 Testimony 17: Holly Wells
389 Testimony 18: James Clouse

PREFACE

This book contains 15-study guide lessons based on the parables of Jesus from the book of Matthew. It then adds two devotions on that parable, two on a parable of Jesus from Mark or Luke, a devotion on a name of Jesus, and finally one on a name of God.

In speaking in parables, Jesus was speaking using an object lesson. A parable is an earthly story used to illustrate a spiritual lesson.

Hopefully, the variety of thoughts will come together to expand your walk with the Lord.

1

THIS LITTLE LIGHT OF MINE
Dr. Randy T. Johnson | Growth Pastor

Light is meant to shine and give direction. In Seminary, for a while, I worked midnights as a Security Officer. One night I was radioed to work with a Police Officer on an armed robbery call. When we arrived in this one dark area, he pulled out his flashlight. It was the state of the art Mag light. It was about two feet long and presumably indestructible. However, that night it did not work. I pulled out my mini mag light. It was only about five inches long, metallic blue, but it worked. We both laughed.

I used to walk through the office structures without turning the lights on. My eyes would adjust, and I would use the moonlight coming through the window or a copy machine that was left on. Any little ray of light helped guide the way and saved me time, as I did not need to go flip the lights on and off. And of course, I had my trusty mini mag flashlight if necessary.

What light sources do you have to use in case of a power outage?
_____
_____
_____

Jesus starts the parables in Matthew during His Sermon on the Mount. In Matthew 5:14-16 He said, *"You are the light of the world. A city set on a hill cannot be hidden. Nor do people light a lamp and put it under a basket, but on a stand, and it gives light to all in the house. In the same way, let your light shine before others, so that they may see your good works and give glory to your Father who is in heaven."*

What is our light that we are to let shine? _____
_____
_____

Why would someone even think of hiding his or her light under a basket? _____
_____
_____

What is the ultimate purpose of our light? _____
_____
_____
_____

Mark 4:21-22 also shares this parable, but with a slight twist, *"And he said to them, 'Is a lamp brought in to be put under a basket, or under a bed, and not on a stand? For nothing is hidden except to be made manifest; nor is anything secret except to come to light.'"*

What elements does Mark add to this parable? _____
_____
_____
_____

What is secret that will come to light? _____
_____
_____

Paul also referred to the analogy of light. In Ephesians 5:8-9 he says, *"For at one time you were darkness, but now you are light in the Lord. Walk as children of light (for the fruit of light is found in all that is good and right and true)."*

How does this passage express our journey with light? _____
_____
_____
_____

Again, Paul referred to light in Philippians 2:15, *"That you may be blameless and innocent, children of God without blemish in the midst of a crooked and twisted generation, among whom you shine as lights in the world."*

How does this verse relate to the topic at hand? _____
_____
_____

Luke records two instances of Jesus giving a parable with the object lesson being that of a light.

First in Luke 8:16-17 He says, *"No one after lighting a lamp covers it with a jar or puts it under a bed, but puts it on a stand, so that those who enter may see the light. For nothing is hidden that will not be made manifest, nor is anything secret that will not be known and come to light."*

Is the light you are shining more of birthday candle or floodlight?
_____
_____
_____

Then in Luke 11:33-36 He says, *"No one after lighting a lamp puts it in a cellar or under a basket, but on a stand, so that those who enter may see the light. Your eye is the lamp of your body. When your eye is healthy, your whole body is full of light, but when it is bad, your body is full of darkness. Therefore be careful lest the light in you be darkness. If then your whole body is full of light, having no part dark, it will be wholly bright, as when a lamp with its rays gives you light."*

Are both references in Luke referring to the same thing? How or how not? _____
_____
_____

Do you think Jesus used the same analogy twice? _____
_____
_____
_____

John 8:12 *("Again Jesus spoke to them, saying, 'I am the light of the world. Whoever follows me will not walk in darkness, but will have the light of life.'")* and 9:5 *("As long as I am in the world, I am the light of the world.")* both call Jesus the "Light of the World."

How are we then able to be called *"the light of the world"* (Matthew 5:14)? _____
_____
_____

As a child, I was raised singing, "This Little Light of Mine."

As we would sing it, we would take our right index finger in the air making a circular motion.

> This little light of mine, I'm gonna let it shine
> This little light of mine, I'm gonna let it shine
> This little light of mine, I'm gonna let it shine
>   Let it shine, Let it shine, Let it shine.

> Hide it under a bushel? No! I'm gonna let it shine
> Hide it under a bushel? No! I'm gonna let it shine
> Hide it under a bushel? No! I'm gonna let it shine
>   Let it shine, Let it shine, Let it shine.

> Don't let Satan blow it out, I'm gonna let it shine
> Don't let Satan blow it out, I'm gonna let it shine
> Don't let Satan blow it out, I'm gonna let it shine
>   Let it shine, Let it shine, Let it shine.

What steps do you need to take in making your light shine brighter? _____
_____
_____

It has been said, "It is better to light a single candle than to curse the darkness."

THIS LITTLE LIGHT OF MINE: DEVOTION 1

THE BUS DRIVER DID IT

Dr. Randy T. Johnson | Growth Pastor

Christians do not do good works to get to Heaven. They strive to do the right thing as a thank you to Jesus for the work He did that allows us to go to Heaven and as a testimony to others of what Jesus can do for them.

As I read Matthew 5:14-16 I realize that Jesus is the Light of the World and that I am to be a light bearer: *"You are the light of the world. A city set on a hill cannot be hidden. Nor do people light a lamp and put it under a basket, but on a stand, and it gives light to all in the house. In the same way, let your light shine before others, so that they may see your good works and give glory to your Father who is in heaven."*

That would have to be one of the biggest compliments ever – people would see our good works, and it would cause them to give glory to God. We are in the right direction when we help those who cannot repay the favor. Visiting prisoners, helping widows and shut-ins, spending time with the fatherless, and just flat out encouraging one another shines a light on a dark world. It confuses people and pushes their focus to God.

Titus 2:7-8 says, *"Show yourself in all respects to be a model of good works, and in your teaching show integrity, dignity, and sound speech that cannot be condemned, so that an opponent may be put to shame, having nothing evil to say about us."* People are always watching. It is ideal to walk in such a way that "the lost" are confounded and ashamed because as they opposed us, they realized they did not have anything bad to say about us.

As I close this devotion, I want to thank someone I never met. I want to thank the bus driver from First Baptist Church of Hazel Park back in the early 1940's who went into Warren and picked up my mom and aunt as little girls and brought them to church. Your good work shined like a light and impacted many lives as they got saved. They have affected thousands, who have impacted thousands, which will impact...

"Preach the Gospel at all times and when necessary use words" (St. Francis of Assisi).

THIS LITTLE LIGHT OF MINE: DEVOTION 2

SALTY "GRAHAM" CRACKER

Dr. Randy T. Johnson | Growth Pastor

The lights of Las Vegas amaze me. You can see them from miles away. It is reported that hotels like the MGM Grand spend $100,000 a month on electricity. I probably do not need to ask who is paying that electric bill.

As we have seen, Matthew 5:14-16 challenges Christians to be a light to the world, *"You are the light of the world. A city set on a hill cannot be hidden. Nor do people light a lamp and put it under a basket, but on a stand, and it gives light to all in the house. In the same way, let your light shine before others, so that they may see your good works and give glory to your Father who is in heaven."*

However, it is beneficial to understand the context. Jesus gives another object lesson right before this section in verse 13, *"You are the salt of the earth, but if salt has lost its taste, how shall its saltiness be restored? It is no longer good for anything except to be thrown out and trampled under people's feet."* The disciples and other listeners would have totally understood the value of salt. Roman soldiers were even paid in salt. I think salt has at least four implications.

First, Christians are to be the salt of the earth in that we are to bring a divine flavor or seasoning into the world. Second, salt is known as a preservative. The world has been preserved because of godly people. Third, salt can sting on a wound, but the goal is to bring healing from sin. Finally, salt was known for stopping decay, and we as Christians should help stop the moral decay of our society.

Yesterday, I put a thank you out to a bus driver I will not meet until Heaven. Today I want to thank a man who is respected by all as a man who knew what it meant to be the salt and light of the world, Billy Graham. When my father was a teenager, he went to a Billy Graham crusade and gave his life to the Lord.

Billy Graham has had an impact on millions of people, and I, fortunately, am one of them.

We are to be salt and light to the world.

"Let your speech always be gracious, seasoned with salt, so that you may know how you ought to answer each person" (Colossians 4:6).

THIS LITTLE LIGHT OF MINE: DEVOTION 3
GOOD SAMARITAN
Dr. Randy T. Johnson | Growth Pastor

As Christians, we are to be salt and light to the world. Jesus uses another parable in Luke to convey this point. It is typically referred to as the parable of the Good Samaritan. Luke 10:25-29 gives the context for the parable. *"And behold, a lawyer stood up to put him to the test, saying, 'Teacher, what shall I do to inherit eternal life?' He said to him, 'What is written in the Law? How do you read it?' And he answered, 'You shall love the Lord your God with all your heart and with all your soul and with all your strength and with all your mind, and your neighbor as yourself.' And he said to him, 'You have answered correctly; do this, and you will live.' But he, desiring to justify himself, said to Jesus, 'And who is my neighbor?'"*

My first impression of looking back at this passage had me surprised on how the lawyer summarized the Law in loving God and loving others. We know from Jesus that this is the right answer. The Lawyer then asks, **"Who is my neighbor?"** It sounds like a simple question.

Jesus tells a story of two well-respected religious men walking right on by a man in need. Then comes "the enemy." This Samaritan takes care of him. Jesus then asks who he thought was neighborly. The Lawyer said, **"The one who showed him mercy."**

Pastor and author Timothy Keller points out the real challenge for us, "We instinctively tend to limit for whom we exert ourselves. We do it for people like us, and for people whom we like. Jesus will have none of that. By depicting a Samaritan helping a Jew,

Jesus could not have found a more forceful way to say that anyone at all in need - regardless of race, politics, class, and religion - is your neighbor. Not everyone is your brother or sister in faith, but everyone is your neighbor, and you must love your neighbor."

Your neighbor is whoever God has cross your path today.

Are you ready and willing to help him or her?

THIS LITTLE LIGHT OF MINE: DEVOTION 4

NOT GOOD ENOUGH SAMARITAN

Dr. Randy T. Johnson | Growth Pastor

Yesterday, we looked at *"Who is my neighbor?"* I wonder if that is the question Jesus was answering. Let's look at the context again in Luke 10:25-29.

"And behold, a lawyer stood up to put him to the test, saying, 'Teacher, what shall I do to inherit eternal life?' He said to him, 'What is written in the Law? How do you read it?' And he answered, 'You shall love the Lord your God with all your heart and with all your soul and with all your strength and with all your mind, and your neighbor as yourself.' And he said to him, 'You have answered correctly; do this, and you will live.' But he, desiring to justify himself, said to Jesus, 'And who is my neighbor?'"

The part that bothers me is the attitude of the lawyer, *"Desiring to justify himself."* Maybe Jesus was addressing the first question, *"What shall I do to inherit eternal life?"*

If loving God and loving others summarizes the Law, and the Law cannot save, then our love (works) is not ever enough.

The lawyer was still trying to justify himself to earn eternal life. I like how Martin Luther King Jr. shows this distinction, "On the parable of the Good Samaritan: I imagine that the first question the priest and Levite asked was: 'If I stop to help this man, what will happen to me?' But by the very nature of his concern, the Good Samaritan reversed the question: 'If I do not stop to help this man, what will happen to him?'"

The focus should not be on our works or us. Our focus should be on God and others. Author William M. Holden was bold in saying, "Hell is paved with good Samaritans." Our works mean nothing. We cannot save ourselves. It is only the work of Jesus Christ that allows salvation.

The lawyer wanted to justify himself. He could not. We cannot.

Love God for who He is and what He has done.

Love others for their sake.

Love others because it pleases God.

"By this all people will know that you are my disciples, if you have love for one another" (John 13:35).

THIS LITTLE LIGHT OF MINE: DEVOTION 5

LIGHT OF THE WORLD

Dr. Randy T. Johnson | Growth Pastor

In John 8 we read the story of the woman caught in adultery. Surprisingly, the scribes and Pharisees worked together and plotted to take down Jesus. Several questions come rushing through my mind. They brought a woman to Him, but where is the man? What did Jesus write in the sand? What did each leader think as they walked away beginning with the oldest ones? What did the by-passers think and how did their emotions and thoughts change? Did Jesus see a broken woman and offer grace by letting her go?

As the questions arise, the main point comes when in the next verse, *"Again Jesus spoke to them, saying, 'I am the light of the world. Whoever follows me will not walk in darkness, but will have the light of life'"* (John 8:12). Jesus is the Light of the World. He could see into the darkness of the scribes and Pharisees' plan. Jesus glanced into their dark paths and brought to light harsh reality. He could see into the life of this sinful yet humiliated woman. He could tell if she was sorry she got caught or truly remorseful. He is the Light of the World.

2 Corinthians 5:21 says, *"For our sake he made him be sin who knew no sin, so that in him we might become the righteousness of God."* As the Light of the World, Jesus never sinned. He calls us to join Him and walk in the light. He challenges and even commands us; *"You shall be holy, for I am holy"* (1 Peter 1:16).

John 8 was not the first time we read of Jesus being associated with light. In John 1:4-5 we read, *"In him was life, and the life was the light of men. The light shines in the darkness, and the darkness has not overcome it."* Light beats darkness every time. Choose to walk in the Light.

Light does not create dust, dirt, or sin. It reveals it. However, as Light of the World, Jesus even worked at the process of purification. Hebrews 1:3 says, ***"He is the radiance of the glory of God and the exact imprint of his nature, and he upholds the universe by the word of his power. After making purification for sins, he sat down at the right hand of the Majesty on high."*** By walking in the Light, we can radiate the glory of God.

I want to close with one of my favorite quotes. It is from the book *Mere Christianity* by C.S. Lewis:

"I am trying here to prevent anyone saying the really foolish thing that people often say about Him: I'm ready to accept Jesus as a great moral teacher, but I don't accept his claim to be God. That is the one thing we must not say. A man who was merely a man and said the sort of things Jesus said would not be a great moral teacher. He would either be a lunatic — on the level with the man who says he is a poached egg — or else he would be the Devil of Hell. You must make your choice. Either this man was, and is, the Son of God, or else a madman or something worse. You can shut him up for a fool, you can spit at him and kill him as a demon or you can fall at his feet and call him Lord and God, but let us not come with any patronizing nonsense about his being a great human teacher. He has not left that open to us. He did not intend to."

Jesus is God. He is the Light of the World.

THIS LITTLE LIGHT OF MINE: DEVOTION 6

THE GOD WHO SEES ME

Dr. Randy T. Johnson | Growth Pastor

Do you ever feel all alone? Do you feel forgotten? Does it seem like no one cares? Hagar felt that way. In Genesis 16:11-14 God reaches out to her at her lowest moment, *"And the angel of the Lord said to her, 'Behold, you are pregnant and shall bear a son. You shall call his name Ishmael, because the Lord has listened to your affliction. He shall be a wild donkey of a man, his hand against everyone and everyone's hand against him, and he shall dwell over against all his kinsmen.' So she called the name of the Lord who spoke to her, 'You are a God of seeing,' for she said, 'Truly here I have seen him who looks after me.' Therefore the well was called Beer-lahai-roi; it lies between Kadesh and Bered."* Her response is interesting. She gives God a name. She calls Him "El Roi" which is translated "the God who sees me." She goes on to name the well "Beer-lahai-roi" which is translated as "the well of Him that lives and sees me."

God sees you. He takes notice. He watches. He cares.

As I have mentioned before, I worked security while attending Seminary. I used to work for two different companies, and it allowed me to work full-time (midnights) and gave me time to study (they loved it as I was one of the few who stayed awake). One night the alarm went off at Baylor College of Dentistry. I was the only one on duty. I had no weapon (I did grab a flashlight). The phone lines were down. It was before everyone carried a phone. I remember going down a stairwell to see what was wrong. The door was open (It was locked earlier). I secured the door and went on. I needed to make my rounds. My heart was pumping overtime. I remember walking through a lobby that had several mirrors. They caught me off guard as I saw several people (who were all me). I admit I am quite the sight at 4:00 am. Even as I walked by the vending machines, everything was quiet until the pop machines compressor turned on. I was ready to swing the flashlight, and I think I would have won that battle. I was a mess. I sat down at my security desk and opened my Bible to Psalm 139. Enjoy verse 7-12:

> *"Where shall I go from your Spirit?*
> *Or where shall I flee from your presence?*
> *If I ascend to heaven, you are there!*
> *If I make my bed in Sheol, you are there!*
> *If I take the wings of the morning*
> *and dwell in the uttermost parts of the sea,*
> *even there your hand shall lead me,*
> *and your right hand shall hold me.*
> *If I say, 'Surely the darkness shall cover me,*
> *and the light about me be night,'*
> *even the darkness is not dark to you;*
> *the night is bright as the day,*
> *for darkness is as light with you."*

It is so comforting to know that God sees us and cares. He loves us, and He is in control. We all had those fears of basements and the stairs that are open for someone or thing to reach through. Do you remember waking up in the night wanting to go to the bathroom, but you were not sure what was under the bed? How about spending the night at grandma's house and hearing noises? We all had and probably even have fears. As we get older, it may be watching a spouse go to serve our country or a child leave for the mission field. It could be driving through a neighborhood or giving our child the car keys.

The next time fear barks, reply with "El Roi!" ***"For God gave us a spirit not of fear but of power and love and self-control"*** (2 Timothy 1:7). The God who sees is watching you. Take control with prayer and Psalm 139.

2

SUCCESS STARTS WITH STRATEGY

Dr. Randy T. Johnson | Growth Pastor

Basketball was my love; baseball was my talent. I still have my first real basketball. My dad found it on the side of the highway. It was leather, the real stuff. I had a hoop in my backyard on an asphalt court. I would do a crossover dribble with the head fake and then hit the fade away jumper of even dunk over my imaginary opponent on my 8' 6" hoop. I was the man.

Do you remember anyone crazy enough to shovel the snow off their court so they could shoot? _____
_____
_____

About the only thing that would stop a true diehard was the ball needed to thaw out or the call for dinner. Sometimes you still played on.

During my childhood years, UCLA and John Wooden were on top of the world. The more you learned about the "Wizard of Westwood," the more you realized he took more pride in changing lives than his ten national championships. Coach Wooden was a man of faith who developed his "Pyramid of Success."

Jesus also talked about success and that the key line of the pyramid was the foundation. Matthew 7:24-27 says, *"Everyone then who hears these words of mine and does them will be like a wise man who built his house on the rock. And the rain fell, and the floods came, and the winds blew and beat on that house, but it did not fall, because it had been founded on the rock. And everyone who hears these words of mine and does not do them will be like a foolish man who built his house on the sand. And the rain fell, and the floods came, and the winds blew and beat against that house, and it fell, and great was the fall of it."*

Have you or someone you know have a building that has had any "structural damage" due to the foundation? _____
_____
_____
_____

Describe Jesus' audience. Who would feel they have the right foundation? _____
_____
_____

What level of commitment is Jesus calling for? _____
_____
_____
_____

Luke 6:47-49
"Everyone who comes to me and hears my words and does them, I will show you what he is like: he is like a man building a house, who dug deep and laid the foundation on the rock. And when a flood arose, the stream broke against

that house and could not shake it, because it had been well built. But the one who hears and does not do them is like a man who built a house on the ground without a foundation. When the stream broke against it, immediately it fell, and the ruin of that house was great."

What details does Luke give that Matthew does not? _____
_____
_____
_____

Do any of these details deepen the meaning for you? _____
_____
_____
_____

The Bible even becomes more specific in describing the Cornerstone of the foundation. It is the starting point. It is pivotal.

Ephesians 2:20-22 says, *"Built on the foundation of the apostles and prophets, Christ Jesus himself being the cornerstone, in whom the whole structure, being joined together, grows into a holy temple in the Lord. In him you also are being built together into a dwelling place for God by the Spirit."*

According to Ephesians, what is the foundation made up of?
_____
_____
_____

What is being built? _____
_____
_____

Acts 4:10-12 is consistent in saying, **"Let it be known to all of you and to all the people of Israel that by the name of Jesus Christ of Nazareth, whom you crucified, whom God raised from the dead—by him this man is standing before you well. This Jesus is the stone that was rejected by you, the builders, which has become the cornerstone. And there is salvation in no one else, for there is no other name under heaven given among men by which we must be saved."**

Are there any other foundations that are suitable? If so, which? If not, how does this passage support that? _____
_____
_____
_____

Psalm 118:22
"The stone that the builders rejected has become the cornerstone."

How could this verse be prophetic in referring to Jesus?
_____
_____
_____

Once the foundation is set, we need to know how to build onto it. On the following page is John Wooden's Pyramid of Success. Even as a coach, notice how he adds faith and patience on the sides.

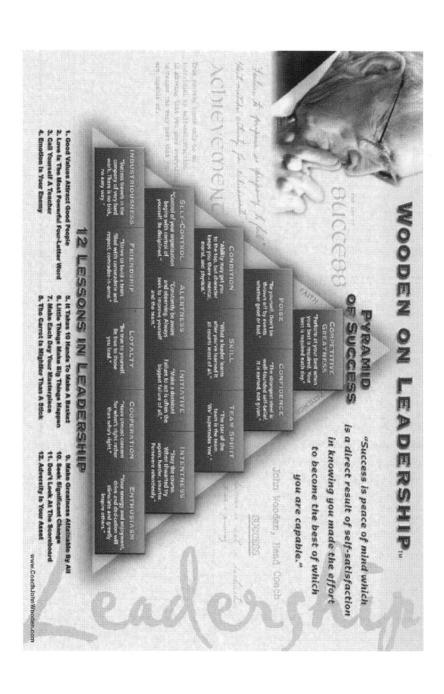

What trait would you add or emphasize more? _____
_____
_____
_____

Which of the twelve Lessons is Leadership jumped out to you?
_____
_____
_____

How would the Be Attitudes (Matthew 5:3-11) and the Fruit of the Spirit (Galatians 5:22-23) fit into your pyramid? _____
_____
_____
_____

"Be more concerned with your character than your reputation, because your character is what you really are, while your reputation is merely what others think you are." John Wooden

"For no one can lay a foundation other than that which is laid, which is Jesus Christ" (1 Corinthians 3:11).

SUCCESS STARTS WITH STRATEGY: DEVOTION 1

HOG HAVEN

Dr. Randy T. Johnson | Growth Pastor

I am not sure the story is true, but it goes something like this: There were these three gravitationally challenged (little) Sus Scrofa Domesticus (pigs) who decided to each build a dwelling. I do not think the fact that they were little plays a part in the story, nor do I believe it is a story about birth order. However, the first "pig" (not intended to be a derogatory term) built his house out of straw and went off to play. Personally, I have not seen pigs play, but that is beside the point. The second "pig" builds his structure out of sticks. I become a little concerned here because although I have beautiful vinyl siding, it is covering a stick built Cape Cod. He too takes to gaming. The third diligent over-achiever painstakingly presses on with bricks. Brick homes are beautiful but can be costly. I can imagine that straw or hay and sticks could be found for free. Where does the third pig get the money for the bricks? Does he make his own? Side note: please do not confuse this pig with the "one that went to the market."

The time comes when the wolf shows up for a house call (it is interesting how often even fairy tales associate a wolf as a dangerous enemy to be avoided). He and his appetite are not welcomed with pigs. The first pig tries to send him away, but he refuses (somehow the straw house had a door that locks). After verbal threats, he huffs and puffs (I think you know this part) and blows the house down. Piggy number one runs to the stick house and is welcomed in with the door shut and locked behind. Since we have accepted the fact that pigs and wolves can talk, we can press on with the story. The same scenario happens with them running to the brick shelter. House number three wins so bacon, sausage, and ham live happily ever after or something like that.

The story is cute, but what about our lives? We set Jesus as the foundation, but what are we building on it each day?

When Jesus was challenged by the "biggest baddest wolf of all time," He responded with Scripture. Jesus limited Himself to the point He needed to study the Word. He then was able to use it to refute the enemy.

Hebrews 4:12 says, ***"For the word of God is living and active, sharper than any two-edged sword, piercing to the division of soul and of spirit, of joints and of marrow, and discerning the thoughts and intentions of the heart."***

Jesus Christ is the foundation. Spending time with Him in reading the Word, meditation, prayer, and gathering with other believers helps strengthen our stand against the storms of life.

"Everyone then who hears these words of mine and does them will be like a wise man who built his house on the rock. And the rain fell, and the floods came, and the winds blew and beat on that house, but it did not fall, because it had been founded on the rock. And everyone who hears these words of mine and does not do them will be like a foolish man who built his house on the sand. And the rain fell, and the floods came, and the winds blew and beat against that house, and it fell, and great was the fall of it" (Matthew 7:24-27).

SUCCESS STARTS WITH STRATEGY: DEVOTION 2

COSTLY STRUCTURAL REPAIRS

Dr. Randy T. Johnson | Growth Pastor

I have had the privilege of visiting the Leaning Tower of Pisa (Yes, I took a picture like I was holding it up). When I visited a few years ago, we were not allowed to climb the steps as it was under construction trying to repair several areas. The tour guide told us there were about 300 steps to the top of the tower, but we could not attempt the climb. I was okay with that as the 294 steps were not on my bucket list.

We learned that the area of Pisa was marshy and other buildings were leaning due to a faulty foundation. Buildings were even sinking. Do not get me wrong; I am always amazed what was built back in the 12th century without any modern equipment and technology. I realize it took some 200 years, but that also impresses me. However, a faulty foundation will eventually be revealed and can be very costly.

We have seen from Matthew 7:24-27 how Matthew described the parable of the men who built their house on rock or sand and the eventual results. Luke describes it this way:

"Everyone who comes to me and hears my words and does them, I will show you what he is like: he is like a man building a house, who dug deep and laid the foundation on the rock. And when a flood arose, the stream broke against that house and could not shake it, because it had been well built. But the one who hears and does not do them is like a man who built a house on the ground without a foundation. When the stream broke against it, immediately it fell, and the ruin of that house was great" (Luke 6:47-49).

I love the story of Paul presenting his case before Agrippa in Acts 26:27-29:

"'King Agrippa, do you believe the prophets? I know that you believe.' And Agrippa said to Paul, 'In a short time would you persuade me to be a Christian?' And Paul said, 'Whether short or long, I would to God that not only you but also all who hear me this day might become such as I am— except for these chains.'"

King Agrippa enters the Coliseum. He might even be carried in and of course, has the best seats in the house. People are jealous. He has whatever he wants. He has power, money, and women. He looks like he has everything.

Paul enters the Coliseum with no money, glamor, or entourage. He is filthy and alone. He does not have political status, women chasing him, or the newest iPhone. He looks like he does not have anything *("except for these chains")*.

Paul sees things differently. He says, *"I would to God that not only you but also all who hear me this day might become such as I am."* Paul brags. Paul saw King Agrippa as the Leaning Tower in its glory days, but he knew the foundation would not hold. He was aware that King Agrippa did not have Jesus and therefore did not have anything. Paul stood there with confidence knowing that the safest place in the world is in the center of God's will. Paul's foundation was sturdy, immovable.

Mark 8:36 says it so well, *"For what does it profit a man to gain the whole world and forfeit his soul?"*

Give your life to Jesus. He gives peace.

SUCCESS STARTS WITH STRATEGY: DEVOTION 3

COUNT THE COST

Dr. Randy T. Johnson | Growth Pastor

"Plan on 20% more time and money than you expected!" A friend told me that 25 years ago when I was having my house built. I tried to explain how I had it all figured out, but he just smiled and said that time would tell. Well, it was not exactly 20%, but it sure cost more than expected and took longer. It is important to plan as well as you can while yet realizing unforeseeable obstacles may and will come.

Luke 14:25-30 gives a parable about building a tower:

"Now great crowds accompanied him, and he turned and said to them, 'If anyone comes to me and does not hate his own father and mother and wife and children and brothers and sisters, yes, and even his own life, he cannot be my disciple. Whoever does not bear his own cross and come after me cannot be my disciple. For which of you, desiring to build a tower, does not first sit down and count the cost, whether he has enough to complete it? Otherwise, when he has laid a foundation and is not able to finish, all who see it begin to mock him, saying, 'This man began to build and was not able to finish.'"

I believe Jesus adds a little humor to His teaching. He talks about the scenario that someone starts making his or her own "statement piece." This structure is to honor them and outlive them, but they cannot finish it due to poor planning. Shame takes over.

I remember seeing a hospital's plans to build a multi-office structure across the street and add a skywalk to it. The building went up quite quickly, and the skywalk was framed, but then everything stopped. They ran out of money. People had to walk outside and cross a busy street. Patients could not be transported because the walkway was unusable. It was a little humorous. Eventually, they were able to raise funds to complete the skywalk.

Proverbs 24:3-4 says, **"By wisdom a house is built, and by understanding it is established; by knowledge the rooms are filled with all precious and pleasant riches."**

Wisdom, understanding, and knowledge proceed to take the step to start building. The same is true in following Jesus. Three times in Luke 14 Jesus says, **"Cannot be my disciple"** (verses 26, 27, 33). Jesus wanted people to know that following Him was not a light decision. He wanted true followers. He wanted (and wants) soldiers. He wanted them to know it would be costly because He was radical. He asked for them to critique their life, direction, dreams, and goals and make sure they were ready.

James 2:17 challenges us by saying, **"So also faith by itself, if it does not have works, is dead."**

I remember sharing the Gospel with a new friend. When I finished, he said, "I do not know if I am ready to make that kind of commitment." I was thrilled. I was so tired of people saying, "I guess so," saying a prayer, and going on as if nothing ever happened. It is as if they are saying, "I guess it cannot hurt." Later, my friend made the decision to truly be a follower of Christ.

Has it cost you anything?

Are you willing to let the Holy Spirit change your life?

Charles Spurgeon summarized this parable well, "True religion is a costly thing. Wisdom suggests that before we enter upon it we should estimate the cost. Cost what it may, it is worth the cost."

It is worth the cost!

SUCCESS STARTS WITH STRATEGY: DEVOTION 4

SOLDIER OF THE KING

Dr. Randy T. Johnson | Growth Pastor

I was raised to never start a fight. I was allowed to defend myself, a friend, or someone who could not defend him or herself. But, I was not to start the fight. Fighting is not a good thing. As I got older, I learned a practical bonus in not starting fights. If you start a fight and lose, you are a total loser; and if you start a fight and win, you are viewed as a bully. You just cannot "win" if you start a fight.

Luke 14:31-33 is a parable about a King analyzing whether or not he should go to war:

"Or what king, going out to encounter another king in war, will not sit down first and deliberate whether he is able with ten thousand to meet him who comes against him with twenty thousand? And if not, while the other is yet a great way off, he sends a delegation and asks for terms of peace. So therefore, any one of you who does not renounce all that he has cannot be my disciple."

We know that one with God is a majority, but we better make sure He is in the fight. Gideon had this conversation as his army of 32,000 shrunk to 10,000 and finally even 300. Gideon was concerned with the cost.

Proverbs 24:5-6 speaks of a similar situation: *"A wise man is full of strength, and a man of knowledge enhances his might, for by wise guidance you can wage your war, and in abundance of counselors there is victory."*

Seeking advice, getting counsel, and counting the cost are crucial for the next big step in life.

Being a soldier of the King comes with a price. We need to be willing to take orders, sacrifice, focus, submit, and put others first. It will affect what you do, where you go, how you speak, what you speak, and totally how you live. It holds the weight of a marriage covenant, but also the respect of such a contract. When married, I want to live a certain way for my bride. It is not a burden. It is a privilege. It is a joy.

2 Timothy 4:7-8 says, **"I have fought the good fight, I have finished the race, I have kept the faith. Henceforth there is laid up for me the crown of righteousness, which the Lord, the righteous judge, will award to me on that Day, and not only to me but also to all who have loved his appearing."**

There is a war, a spiritual battle all around us.

Who is your commander?

Can He count on you?

SUCCESS STARTS WITH STRATEGY: DEVOTION 5

JESUS ROCKS!

Dr. Randy T. Johnson | Growth Pastor

My family is a dog family. We have had two Golden Retrievers, and both of our children have one now. They are so loyal and loving. It is interesting to listen to people who are searching for their next "best friend." They drive all over to see the puppies. They research the breeder. They look for the best deal and often brag how inexpensive he or she was. However, no matter how good of a deal you received, having a dog is costly. Puppy breath is precious but the time and cost involved in having an animal need to be considered. If the price of the dog concerns you, then you definitely cannot afford one because the ongoing costs will surprise you. Count the cost.

Paul challenges believers, *"So, whether you eat or drink, or whatever you do, do all to the glory of God"* (1 Corinthians 10:31). Every choice in our life should be weighed in how it brings glory to God.

This week we started by studying the parable of the men who built on foundations of sand and rock. That foundation is even further strengthened and defined when we realize Jesus is the Chief Cornerstone!

Psalm 118:22
"The stone that the builders rejected has become the cornerstone."

Ephesians 2:20
"Built on the foundation of the apostles and prophets, Christ Jesus himself being the cornerstone."

1 Corinthians 3:11
"For no one can lay a foundation other than that which is laid, which is Jesus Christ."

Pastor Jim Combs gives a pretty simple process in spending money. First, give to the Lord. Give out of your "first fruits" a tithe or amount back to the Lord. Second, provide for your family. Food, clothing, medical needs, shelter, transportation, future planning, and the sort are necessary for providing for those God is placed in our life. Third, use the money for yourself. Have a hobby. Enjoy life. God smiles when we enjoy His creation.

This process places Jesus as the Chief Cornerstone of our life. Everything builds off that pivotal point in our foundation. Our decisions from buying a house, car (new or used), bike or Bike, gaming system, new phone, or even a dog should be thought and prayed through the grid of how it builds on the foundation. It should also affect where we go, what we do, and with whom we spend time.

"Whatever you do, do all to the glory of God."

What area in your life are you holding on to right now?

Give it to God. He has something better for you. He has the upgrade!

SUCCESS STARTS WITH STRATEGY: DEVOTION 6

GOD ALMIGHTY

Dr. Randy T. Johnson | Growth Pastor

In 1982 Amy Grant came out with a hit single entitled, "El Shaddai." It was acknowledged as the Gospel Song of the Year.

> El Shaddai, El Shaddai; El-elyon na Adonai
> Age to age you're still the same
> By the power of the name
> El Shaddai, El Shaddai; Erkamka na Adonai
> We will praise and lift You high
> El Shaddai
> Through Your love and the ram
> You saved the son of Abraham
> Through the power of Your hand
> Turned the sea into dry land
> To the outcast on her knees
> You were the God who really sees
> And by Your might
> You set Your children free

El Shaddai means "God Almighty." God is called "Almighty" forty-eight times in Scripture, but is only referred to as "God Almighty" seven times. To me, it seems redundant. Of course, He is Almighty; He is God! Redundancy has value in emphasizing a point. He is God Almighty.

One of the seven usages of El Shaddai is in Genesis 17:1-4:

"When Abram was ninety-nine years old the Lord appeared to Abram and said to him, 'I am God Almighty; walk before me, and be blameless, that I may make my covenant between me and you, and may multiply you greatly.' Then Abram

fell on his face. And God said to him, 'Behold, my covenant is with you, and you shall be the father of a multitude of nations.'"

God tells old man Abram that he will have a son, even a whole nation. He tells him that a king, even the King of Kings, will come from his lineage. He says He will protect them from their enemies, even though they would often be a nation without a land. God will provide and protect. He is the God Almighty.

God Almighty makes a covenant with Abraham (in verse five God changes Abram's name to Abraham).

Notice Abram's response to God Almighty. He fell on his face. I know there are those who think God created everything and then sat back in a lounge chair, drinks some sweet tea, and watches everything go by in our lives. That is so sad. God is active in the world today. He is working through His people. It should humble us to the point that we regularly fall down on our face and acknowledge that He is God Almighty.

An interesting note: The word for Almighty appears to come from the Hebrew word for mountain. This week we have discussed having a solid foundation. It is the mountain. It is God Almighty.

When was the last time you fell on your face honoring Him because He is the God Almighty?

The next time you fall on your face in life, remember there is a God Almighty.

3

NEW COVENANT

Dr. Randy T. Johnson | Growth Pastor

A few years ago I had patches made for my golf team. The guys liked it. We designed our own logo. We bought expensive pullover golf jackets and had the patch sewn on the left sleeve. We expected other teams to be a little jealous. We wanted to set the standard. Then we washed the jackets. I am not sure if the patches were cheap or if I should have prewashed (and dried) the jackets, but they sure did not look right.

I messed up a pretty simple parable. Matthew 9:16-17 (Mark 2:21-22 and Luke 5:36-38) records some basic common sense:

"No one puts a piece of unshrunk cloth on an old garment, for the patch tears away from the garment, and a worse tear is made."

Have you ever made the mistake of trying to "patch" a hole with the wrong material? _____
_____
_____
_____

Do you remember a fun patch you had as a kid? What was it, what did it say, and what was it put on? _____

_____

_____

_____

Jesus uses the same basic principle but relates it to another object:

"Neither is new wine put into old wineskins. If it is, the skins burst and the wine is spilled and the skins are destroyed. But new wine is put into fresh wineskins, and so both are preserved."

Wineskins were often animal intestines (does that sound appetizing?). The fermented wine would cause them to expand. After a while, they would harden and not be as pliable. They were still useful for water, but could not handle any more expanding. If someone put fresh wine in any old wineskin, it would burst. Both the wineskin and the wine would be lost.

Both of these parables have a sense of logic to them. It has been said that the problem with common sense is that it is not common. Jesus is giving good household advice so that you can protect your items from tearing or breaking. However, these parables have a sense of value to them. You do not want to waste and lose good things.

What was Jesus really saying with these parables? _____

_____

_____

_____

The context sheds more light. Matthew 9:14-15 says,

"Then the disciples of John came to him, saying, 'Why do we and the Pharisees fast, but your disciples do not fast?' And Jesus said to them, 'Can the wedding guests mourn as long as the bridegroom is with them? The days will come when the bridegroom is taken away from them, and then they will fast.'"

Who is the "bridegroom?" _____
_____
_____

Who were the "wedding guests?" _____
_____
_____

Jesus brought a New Covenant.

What was the old covenant? What did it entail? _____
_____
_____
_____
_____

The New Covenant fulfilled over 300 prophecies (Josh McDowell says there are about 330 Old Testament prophecies fulfilled in Jesus).

Are you surprised at the number of prophecies God gave us in the Old Testament so people could recognize the Messiah?
_____
_____
_____
_____

The New Covenant is built on some specific blocks. Dr. Norman Geisler lists fourteen essential doctrines (set of beliefs) that are fundamental to Christianity. If any one of these doctrines is false, it breaks the whole chain.

1. There is only one God.

John 17:3
"And this is eternal life, that they know you the only true God, and Jesus Christ whom you have sent."

Deuteronomy 6:4
"Hear, O Israel: The Lord our God, the Lord is one."

Is the statement that there is just one God arrogant, intolerant, and closed-minded? _____
_____
_____
_____

What is implied when someone says they believe a certain thing?
_____
_____
_____
_____

Can there be absolute truth? _____
_____
_____
_____
_____

2. God's trinity is also referred to as a tri-unity.

The Father is called God.

2 Thessalonians 1:2
"Grace to you and peace from God our Father and the Lord Jesus Christ."

The Son (Jesus) is called God.

John 1:1-3
"In the beginning was the Word, and the Word was with God, and the Word was God. He was in the beginning with God. All things were made through him, and without him was not any thing made that was made."

John 10:30
"I and the Father are one."

The Holy Spirit is called God.

Acts 5:3-4
"But Peter said, 'Ananias, why has Satan filled your heart to lie to the Holy Spirit and to keep back for yourself part of the proceeds of the land? While it remained unsold, did it not remain your own? And after it was sold, was it not at your disposal? Why is it that you have contrived this deed in your heart? You have not lied to man but God.'"

Does Scripture support all three being God? _____
_____
_____
_____

Matthew 28:19
"Go therefore and make disciples of all nations, baptizing them in the name of the Father and of the Son and of the Holy Spirit."

Do you have an object lesson that helps you picture the concept of the Trinity (i.e. An egg, banana, or river)? _____
_____
_____
_____
_____

3. We have all sinned.

Romans 3:10-11
"As it is written: 'None is righteous, no, not one; no one understands; no one seeks for God.'"

Romans 3:23
"For all have sinned and fall short of the glory of God."

Do you believe people are innately good or evil? _____
_____
_____
_____
_____

4. Christ was born of a virgin.

Isaiah 7:14

"Therefore the Lord himself will give you a sign. Behold, the virgin shall conceive and bear a son, and shall call his name Immanuel."

Why is it important that Jesus did not have a biological (earthly) father? _____
_____
_____
_____

5. Christ never sinned.

2 Corinthians 5:21

"For our sake he made him to be sin who knew no sin, so that in him we might become the righteousness of God."

Hebrews 4:15

"For we do not have a high priest who is unable to sympathize with our weaknesses, but one who in every respect has been tempted as we are, yet without sin."

Since Jesus was man, could He sin – or – since He was God was it impossible for Him to sin (Please don't spend too long on this one)? _____
_____
_____
_____

How is temptation different from sin? _____
_____
_____
_____
_____

6. Jesus is God.

John 1:1
"In the beginning was the Word, and the Word was with God, and the Word was God."

Colossians 2:9
"For in him the whole fullness of deity dwells bodily."

When did Jesus begin? What is His starting point? _____
_____
_____
_____
_____

7. Jesus is man.

Philippians 2:7-8
"But emptied himself, by taking the form of a servant, being born in the likeness of men. And being found in human form, he humbled himself by becoming obedient to the point of death, even death on a cross."

What aspect of Jesus being "man" is most comforting to you?
_____
_____
_____

8. Man needs God's grace. It is unearned favor of God.

Ephesians 2:8-9
"For by grace you have been saved through faith. And this is not your own doing; it is the gift of God, not a result of works, so that no one may boast."

Romans 9:16
"So then it depends not on human will or exertion, but on God, who has mercy."

Why do anything good if it will not get us to Heaven? _____
_____
_____
_____
_____

9. Faith is necessary. Faith is complete trust and confidence in someone or something.

Ephesians 2:8-9
"For by grace you have been saved through faith. And this is not your own doing; it is the gift of God, not a result of works, so that no one may boast."

Hebrews 11:6
"And without faith it is impossible to please him, for whoever would draw near to God must believe that he exists and that he rewards those who seek him."

What illustration do you like for faith (i.e. chair, Niagara Falls)?
_____
_____
_____
_____

10. Christ's death atoned for our sin. Atoning is to make restitution for something. It is to pay for or make good.

Mark 10:45
"For even the Son of Man came not to be served but to serve, and to give his life as a ransom for many."

What does the word ransom mean? _____
_____
_____
_____

Who was the ransom paid to? Why? _____
_____
_____
_____

11. Christ rose again in bodily form.

Romans 4:25
"Who was delivered up for our trespasses and raised for our justification."

Luke 24:39
"See my hands and my feet, that it is I myself. Touch me, and see. For a spirit does not have flesh and bones as you see that I have."

How long did Jesus remain on earth after His resurrection (Acts 1:3)? Why? _____
_____
_____
_____

12.   Christ's ascension was in bodily form.

John 16:7
"Nevertheless, I tell you the truth: it is to your advantage that I go away, for if I do not go away, the Helper will not come to you. But if I go, I will send him to you."

Acts 1:9-10
"And when he had said these things, as they were looking on, he was lifted up, and a cloud took him out of their sight. And while they were gazing into heaven as he went, behold, two men stood by them in white robes."

Who is the Helper? How is it better having the Helper than having Jesus still on earth? _____
_____
_____
_____

13.   Jesus prays (intercedes) for believers.

Hebrews 7:25
"Consequently, he is able to save to the uttermost those who draw near to God through him, since he always lives to make intercession for them."

1 John 2:1

"My little children, I am writing these things to you so that you may not sin. But if anyone does sin, we have an advocate with the Father, Jesus Christ the righteous."

What do you want Jesus to pray for you? _____
_____
_____
_____
_____

14. Christ is coming again.

Revelation 22:12

"Behold, I am coming soon, bringing my recompense with me, to repay each one for what he has done."

Luke 12:40

"You also must be ready, for the Son of Man is coming at an hour you do not expect."

Is there anything you want to change in your life before Jesus makes a surprise visit? What, how, and when will you take action?
_____
_____
_____

"Most Christians are still living with an Old Testament view of their heart. Jeremiah 17:9 says, 'My heart is deceitfully wicked.' No, it's not. Not after the work of Christ, because the promise of the new covenant is a new heart." John Eldredge (Christian author)

NEW COVENANT: DEVOTION 1

LIBERAL OR LEGALIST

Dr. Randy T. Johnson | Growth Pastor

Matthew 9:16-17 gives the parable of "out with the old and in with the new:"
"No one puts a piece of unshrunk cloth on an old garment, for the patch tears away from the garment, and a worse tear is made. Neither is new wine put into old wineskins. If it is, the skins burst and the wine is spilled and the skins are destroyed. But new wine is put into fresh wineskins, and so both are preserved."

The parable is an object lesson to explain that Jesus brought a New Covenant. It should not have caught them totally off guard because Jeremiah 31:31-33 spoke of it:

"Behold, the days are coming, declares the Lord, when I will make a new covenant with the house of Israel and the house of Judah, not like the covenant that I made with their fathers on the day when I took them by the hand to bring them out of the land of Egypt, my covenant that they broke, though I was their husband, declares the Lord. For this is the covenant that I will make with the house of Israel after those days, declares the Lord: I will put my law within them, and I will write it on their hearts. And I will be their God, and they shall be my people."

The Old Covenant was about the Law and actions while the New Covenant speaks of the heart and God's grace. Even today we see people struggle over the works and grace move.

Pastor Jim Combs spoke a very practical and pointed message that relates to this issue. He was talking from Revelation 22:18-19:

"I warn everyone who hears the words of the prophecy of this book: if anyone adds to them, God will add to him the plagues described in this book, and if anyone takes away from the words of the book of this prophecy, God will take away his share in the tree of life and in the holy city, which are described in this book."

Pastor Jim merely summarized this passage by saying if you add anything (i.e. rules) to Scripture you are a legalist and if you remove anything from Scripture you are a liberal.

We need to enjoy God's grace and be careful of creating rules and a lifestyle to "earn" God's love. Let's enjoy His presence and walk in His ways.

NEW COVENANT: DEVOTION 2

LICENSE TO SIN

Dr. Randy T. Johnson | Growth Pastor

We have spent a couple of lessons on Matthew 9:16-17 which contains the parable of "out with the old and in with the new:"

"No one puts a piece of unshrunk cloth on an old garment, for the patch tears away from the garment, and a worse tear is made. Neither is new wine put into old wineskins. If it is, the skins burst and the wine is spilled and the skins are destroyed. But new wine is put into fresh wineskins, and so both are preserved."

The Old Covenant was about the Law and actions while the New Covenant speaks of the heart and God's grace. Even today we see people struggle over the works and grace move.

Some become legalists and live under an old regime of fear; however, others swing the pendulum too far and strut their "Christian freedom." Their bumper sticker says, "Christians are not perfect, only forgiven." Although I agree with the statement, I sense that some go into sin with the mindset that it is no big deal because they will be forgiven. They lighten the weight of sin. They use their Christian freedom as an excuse to sin. 1 Peter 2:16 says, *"Live as people who are free, not using your freedom as a cover-up for evil, but living as servants of God."*

This excuse to sin becomes a license to sin.

We need to be Christians – Christ-like or little Christ. We should strive to be a "mini-me" of Jesus. 1 John 1:6 says, *"If we say we have fellowship with him while we walk in darkness, we lie*

and do not practice the truth." Intentional sin, with no sense of guilt, means someone may be lying to him or herself in thinking that their relationship with God is secure.

1 Corinthians 10:31 should be our motto, ***"So, whether you eat or drink, or whatever you do, do all to the glory of God."*** We need to walk in such a way that thinks of others. Our life may be the only Bible some people may ever read. They should see selflessness. This is not for us to think less of our self (we are always a child of God), it is a challenge for us to think of our self, less.

We should be willing to sacrifice personal gratification in loyalty to Jesus, the Groom. We as part of the Church are His Bride. It should be a relationship based on love, truth, and faithfulness.

"Until death do us ... unite, forever."

NEW COVENANT: DEVOTION 3

SULTAN OF SWAT

Dr. Randy T. Johnson | Growth Pastor

When I was in high school my grandmother, who lived across the street, came outside to speak to me. My mom and I were in the yard. Grandma told me she found a baseball in the attic that was grandpas. He died when I was four, but she was convinced he would want me to have it. I thanked her, but she continued by saying someone signed it. I know this is sounding like a movie, but it actually happened to me. I asked my grandmother if she knew who signed it. She said, "Baby something?" I looked at my mom who was a big baseball fan and knew every Tiger and most other key players throughout history. Mom said, "Grandpa was a big fan." I said, "Grandma, could it be Babe Ruth?" She said, "Maybe. Was he good? Grandpa said the guy was good." I walked across the street to get the real thing. Babe Ruth and a couple of other Hall of Famers signed it. I still have it and even bought a special container with museum glass to protect it. She even had pictures that my aunt took of Babe, Bill Dickie, and Walter Johnson. I then collected some other sports' memorabilia. Sometimes going to a card show would consume me.

Luke 12:16-21 records a parable that shows how priorities can get out of line:

"And he told them a parable, saying, 'The land of a rich man produced plentifully, and he thought to himself, 'What shall I do, for I have nowhere to store my crops?' And he said, 'I will do this: I will tear down my barns and build larger ones, and there I will store all my grain and my goods. And I will say to my soul, 'Soul, you have ample goods laid up for many years; relax, eat, drink, be merry.'

But God said to him, 'Fool! This night your soul is required of you, and the things you have prepared, whose will they be?' So is the one who lays up treasure for himself and is not rich toward God."

The rich man put his trust in something that was not secure. He thought material goods were the end goal. Matthew 6:19-21 says, *"Do not lay up for yourselves treasures on earth, where moth and rust destroy and where thieves break in and steal, but lay up for yourselves treasures in heaven, where neither moth nor rust destroys and where thieves do not break in and steal. For where your treasure is, there your heart will be also."* Several individuals in Scripture were wealthy and godly (Abraham, Joseph, Job, David, and Lydia). They owned their possessions; their possessions did not own them.

When I received the Babe Ruth ball, I immediately went and showed it to a friend. He threw it to his brother. It was a horrible throw that scraped across the sidewalk. I was ready to pound him. The ball became more important than a friend.

Are you laying up treasures in Heaven or on earth?

Do you have a hobby that is getting out of hand?

NEW COVENANT: DEVOTION 4

CRAWL LIKE A CAMEL

Dr. Randy T. Johnson | Growth Pastor

I have had the privilege of visiting Israel twice. The first time I went with a group of pastors. The second trip I took a group of high school students and some of their parents. My son went (he was going into 9th grade), and I was able to baptize him in the Jordan River. It was a spiritual highlight for me.

The parable we looked at yesterday (Luke 12:16-21) about a man storing up earthly treasures only to lose his life that night, reminds me of another Bible story. In Matthew 19 a young man asks Jesus about eternal life. They talk about the Ten Commandments and then *"Jesus said to him, 'If you would be perfect, go, sell what you possess and give to the poor, and you will have treasure in heaven; and come, follow me'"* (verse 21). The man goes away sad because he was wealthy. His possessions and money were too important to him. It lines right up with yesterday's parable, *"So is the one who lays up treasure for himself and is not rich toward God"* (Luke 12:21).

Back in Matthew 19, an intriguing object lesson is given, *"And Jesus said to his disciples, 'Truly, I say to you, only with difficulty will a rich person enter the kingdom of heaven. Again I tell you, it is easier for a camel to go through the eye of a needle than for a rich person to enter the kingdom of God'"* (verses 23-24). How can a camel go through an eye of a needle? They cannot. So, that would mean no one who is wealthy could ever go to Heaven. That does not sound right.

So, when I was in Israel there were men with their camels at every major tourist sight offering a ride for a price. I asked several people if their camel could crawl. They laughed at me. Finally, at Qumran, where the Dead Sea Scrolls were found in the caves, a man told me his could. He told me the others could not because they have nice barns, but he is not that fortunate, and his camel escapes the weather by going into a cave. The entrance is critical, so his camel gets down on his knees (actually called palms) and crawls in.

There was an entrance, or gateway, in Jerusalem called the eye of the needle. Camels had to have everything taken off of them and then they could crawl through the opening. They were stripped of everything.

Are we willing to humbly bow before God realizing our earthly treasures do not impress Him?

Are we building for Heaven?

We need to use our resources, talents, time, and energy to make a difference forever.

NEW COVENANT: DEVOTION 5

LAMB OF GOD

Dr. Randy T. Johnson | Growth Pastor

My mom loved giraffes. I am not sure what the fascination was, but if I ever saw a giraffe figurine, I would consider getting it for her. Even now when I see anything in a giraffe motif, I think of her. She had them all over the house. My dad's favorite animal was the tiger. My mom even called him Tommy Tiger. I guess it would make sense if mine were the "bald" eagle.

Scripture has a special animal associated with Jesus. It is the lamb. John the Baptist immediately made the connection, *"The next day he saw Jesus coming toward him, and said, 'Behold, the Lamb of God, who takes away the sin of the world!'"* (John 1:29). In verse 36 he again states, *"And he looked at Jesus as he walked by and said, 'Behold, the Lamb of God!'"* John the Baptist knew the Messiah was coming and that He would be the sacrificial lamb to cover our sin. No longer would we need to sacrifice animals to appease God. Jesus, the Messiah, did it once and for all.

Peter also acknowledges the sacrifice of Christ being like that of a Passover lamb:

"Knowing that you were ransomed from the futile ways inherited from your forefathers, not with perishable things such as silver or gold, but with the precious blood of Christ, like that of a lamb without blemish or spot" (1 Peter 1:18-19).

By the way, the Lamb is not finished with us. John records in Revelation 5:6-12 a further description:

"And between the throne and the four living creatures and among the elders I saw a Lamb standing, as though it had been slain, with seven horns and with seven eyes, which are the seven spirits of God sent out into all the earth. And he went and took the scroll from the right hand of him who was seated on the throne. And when he had taken the scroll, the four living creatures and the twenty-four elders fell down before the Lamb, each holding a harp, and golden bowls full of incense, which are the prayers of the saints. And they sang a new song, saying,
'Worthy are you to take the scroll and to open its seals, for you were slain, and by your blood you ransomed people for God from every tribe and language and people and nation, and you have made them a kingdom and priests to our God, and they shall reign on the earth.' Then I looked, and I heard around the throne and the living creatures and the elders the voice of many angels, numbering myriads of myriads and thousands of thousands, saying with a loud voice, 'Worthy is the Lamb who was slain, to receive power and wealth and wisdom and might and honor and glory and blessing!'"

We were saved by the Lamb.

He is worthy of all we have: our allegiance, finances, strength, dreams, and worship.

Giraffe, tiger, bald eagle, or whatever animal you love, be careful not to be a leader dog. We are the ones who need Someone to guide us.

NEW COVENANT: DEVOTION 6

YHWH

Dr. Randy T. Johnson | Growth Pastor

Change can be difficult for me. I like order, structure, and even a little predictability. Therefore, ties can bother me. It is not just because I have a nineteen and a half-inch neck; it is because just when I get a nice selection of ties, fashion changes. It seems like every ten years the width of ties changes. When I was young, it seemed like there was a normal width. (Yes, I lived during the leisure suit times with no tie. It was "groovy.") Then came the wide ties. They were so wide I believe you could have worn just a collar without a shirt and no one would know. I do not know if I should admit how flowery they became. Now we are into the thin tie. It is not the best thing for a guy my size. Finally, there is the bowtie. It used to be just for weddings and black-tie occasions, but now it is pretty standard. I know the changes are financially motivated by the "fashion" world.

Change can leave a lot of people unsettled.

God does not change. YHWH or Yahweh is the most commonly used name for God. It is used about 7,000 times in the Bible. He is the great "I AM." He is "The One Who is." He is not just one who was or one who will be. He is! Athletes are often ranked against others. Some are viewed as has-beens while others "have not reached their potential yet." God is different. He always "is." He has no beginning and no end. He is not getting better or wearing down. He is!

God names Himself in Exodus 3:14, **"God said to Moses, 'I am who I am.' And he said, 'Say this to the people of Israel, 'I am has sent me to you.'"** The God who always has been was with Moses. The God who always has been is with you. He has not changed. People change, God does not.

Malachi 3:6 says, *"For I the Lord do not change; therefore you, O children of Jacob, are not consumed."*

God never changes. He can be trusted. He is not moody. He is predictable. He is love. He is forgiving. He is just. He is merciful. He is!

Just as I try to get used to the width of ties, I am told there are different knots for neckties. My friend, Jared, started showing me several that he used. There is the Windsor knot, the Half-Windsor knot, Four-in-Hand knot, St Andrew knot, Victoria knot, and even the Trinity knot. They are very cool looking and unique. I then had to figure out how common this was. I found an article from Popular Science (2014) stating that Mikael Vejdemo-Johansson, a mathematician in Stockholm, came up with 177,147 different ways to tie the knot of a necktie. It was an official study (Can you say, "Get a life?"). The next time you see me in a tie, it will be a basic old school knot.

Fashions change; God does not.

4

SOWERS KNEEDED

Dr. Randy T. Johnson | Growth Pastor

I do not have a green thumb. I think I could kill a plastic plant. I tried to research what the antonym for a green thumb was, and it appears it can be brown, black, red, or a picture of my hands. It was important for me to learn the difference between annual and perennial. Each May for Mother's Day and our Anniversary I buy five new hanging planters and two trays of flowers to decorate our front stationary planters. I often have to replace a "perennial," too. Both my wife and I appreciate the blooming flowers.

Matthew 13 records the parable of the sower. He seems to have some insight on planting.

Matthew 13:3-9
"And he told them many things in parables, saying: 'A sower went out to sow. And as he sowed, some seeds fell along the path, and the birds came and devoured them. Other seeds fell on rocky ground, where they did not have much soil, and immediately they sprang up, since they had no depth of soil, but when the sun rose they were scorched. And since they had no root, they withered away. Other seeds fell among thorns, and the thorns grew up and choked them.

Other seeds fell on good soil and produced grain, some a hundredfold, some sixty, some thirty. He who has ears, let him hear.'"

Who is telling the parable? _____
_____
_____

Who is the sower? _____
_____
_____

What is the seed? _____
_____
_____

What are the four kinds of soil? _____
_____
_____
_____
_____

What is the result from these soils? _____
_____
_____
_____
_____

Matthew 13:10-13

"Then the disciples came and said to him, 'Why do you speak to them in parables?' And he answered them, 'To you it has been given to know the secrets of the kingdom of heaven, but to them it has not been given. For to the one who has, more

will be given, and he will have an abundance, but from the one who has not, even what he has will be taken away. This is why I speak to them in parables, because seeing they do not see, and hearing they do not hear, nor do they understand.'"

What is the purpose of an object lesson? _____
_____
_____

Why did Jesus use parables? _____
_____
_____

How does verse 12 relate to the parable of talents? _____
_____
_____

Matthew 13:14-17
"Indeed, in their case the prophecy of Isaiah is fulfilled that says:
'You will indeed hear but never understand,
  and you will indeed see but never perceive.
For this people's heart has grown dull,
  and with their ears they can barely hear,
  and their eyes they have closed,
lest they should see with their eyes
  and hear with their ears
and understand with their heart
  and turn, and I would heal them.'
But blessed are your eyes, for they see, and your ears, for they hear. For truly, I say to you, many prophets and righteous people longed to see what you see, and did not see it, and to hear what you hear, and did not hear it."

Who was given much, but ignored what they saw and heard?
_____
_____
_____

Who was seeking and longing for more? _____
_____
_____

Matthew 13:18-23

"Hear then the parable of the sower: When anyone hears the word of the kingdom and does not understand it, the evil one comes and snatches away what has been sown in his heart. This is what was sown along the path. As for what was sown on rocky ground, this is the one who hears the word and immediately receives it with joy, yet he has no root in himself, but endures for a while, and when tribulation or persecution arises on account of the word, immediately he falls away. As for what was sown among thorns, this is the one who hears the word, but the cares of the world and the deceitfulness of riches choke the word, and it proves unfruitful. As for what was sown on good soil, this is the one who hears the word and understands it. He indeed bears fruit and yields, in one case a hundredfold, in another sixty, and in another thirty."

Who is the sower? _____
_____
_____

What is the seed? _____
_____
_____

What are the four kinds of soil? _____
_____
_____
_____
_____

What is the result from these soils? What was their "enemy"?
_____
_____
_____
_____

Which "soils" are actually saved? _____
_____
_____

What is the responsibility of the sower? _____
_____
_____

What is the responsibility of the soil? _____
_____
_____

Who has the larger responsibility, the sower or the soil?
_____
_____
_____

How does this parable define our evangelistic plan? _____
_____
_____
_____

What should be our follow-up plan when we see someone get saved? _____
_____
_____

"This first parable establishes the basic character of the present age, awaiting the return of the rejected King. The age will include some who believe, many who will not believe." John Walvoord

Will more people go to Heaven or Hell? _____
_____
_____

List some people in your life you are not sure will go to Heaven?
_____
_____
_____

What will you do? _____
_____
_____

Normally the best way to plant seeds is to start on your knees.

SOWERS KNEEDED: DEVOTION 1

DIRTY HANDS

Dr. Randy T. Johnson | Growth Pastor

I have learned that timing is critical when planting. Plants have tags that explain for what zone they are best suited. It is also important to know the last and first frost for the hardiness of a plant. I am not sure the best times, but I know enough to check it out.

Karen and Mike Garofalo put together some points in Garden Digest that I can relate to:
1. The only way to ensure rain is to give the garden a good soaking.
2. Weeds grow at precisely the rate you pull them out.
3. Nothing ever looks like it does on the seed packet.
4. The only way to guarantee some color all year round is to buy a garden gnome.
5. However bare the lawn, grass will appear in the cracks between the patio paving stones.
6. Evergreens go a funny shade of brown in the winter.

Continuing with the garden theme, Mark 4 also records the parable of the sower and the seed. Jesus gives His explanation in verses 14-20:

"The sower sows the word. And these are the ones along the path, where the word is sown: when they hear, Satan immediately comes and takes away the word that is sown in them. And these are the ones sown on rocky ground: the ones who, when they hear the word, immediately receive it with joy. And they have no root in themselves, but endure for a while; then, when tribulation or persecution arises on account of the word, immediately they fall away. And others are the ones sown among thorns. They are those who hear the word, but the cares of the world and the

deceitfulness of riches and the desires for other things enter in and choke the word, and it proves unfruitful. But those that were sown on the good soil are the ones who hear the word and accept it and bear fruit, thirtyfold and sixtyfold and a hundredfold."

As I read through the parable, it made me wonder who is more responsible for the truth: the sower or the soil?

Like the sower, not only is timing critical for planting but also one needs to work the ground. I cannot just throw the seed (Word) around aimlessly hoping something sticks. I need to take some responsibility.

2 Timothy 4:2 says, *"Preach the word; be ready in season and out of season; reprove, rebuke, and exhort, with complete patience and teaching."* Like the sower, I need to be always ready. It takes work hard. There is a time for patience, but there is time for us to step out and press forward.

I, as a witness for Jesus Christ, need to get my hands dirty. I need to go to the soil. I need to work it and even break it down. I want to do everything possible to make sure the seed (Word) is well received. Then I need to look for more fields.

Paul says, *"I planted, Apollos watered, but God gave the growth. So neither he who plants nor he who waters is anything, but only God who gives the growth. He who plants and he who waters are one, and each will receive his wages according to his labor. For we are God's fellow workers. You are God's field, God's building"* (1 Corinthians 3:6-9).

Let us team up. One plants, while the other waters. Then we can watch together what God is doing.

SOWERS KNEEDED: DEVOTION 2

TWELVE INCHES

Dr. Randy T. Johnson | Growth Pastor

Twenty-five years ago my wife and I bought a beautiful acre and a half in Auburn Hills. It even backs up to forty acres of protected wetland. The back half of the property was dense woods while there was seasonal water in the front corner. We put a fire pit and dirt bike paths in the back but kept the forest. In the front, we brought in hundreds of yards of "clean fill" dirt. My father helped me clear the property for the house. We spent hours together.

The "clean fill" had a lot of clay. It is hard to grow anything worthwhile in clay. It is important to start with good soil. In viewing the sower and the seed again, I want to focus on the soil.

Even Luke recorded the parable of the sower and the seed. It must have been an important parable for it to be registered three times in Scripture. Luke 8:11-15 says,

"Now the parable is this: The seed is the word of God. The ones along the path are those who have heard; then the devil comes and takes away the word from their hearts, so that they may not believe and be saved. And the ones on the rock are those who, when they hear the word, receive it with joy. But these have no root; they believe for a while, and in time of testing fall away. And as for what fell among the thorns, they are those who hear, but as they go on their way they are choked by the cares and riches and pleasures of life, and their fruit does not mature. As for that in the good soil, they are those who, hearing the word, hold it fast in an honest and good heart, and bear fruit with patience."

The seed is the Word of God, and you are the soil. Someone has shared the Word of God, so what have you done with it? Were you excited at first and then fizzled out? Did you get caught up in an old lifestyle or habits? Did bad influences pull you back? Did you walk away from the Word?

Acts 17:11 shows a group who received the Word and then continued to study it daily:

"Now these Jews were more noble than those in Thessalonica; they received the word with all eagerness, examining the Scriptures daily to see if these things were so."

There is an adage that some people miss Heaven by twelve inches. They hear the Word and think about it, but it never sinks into their heart or being. They do not let the seed grow.

What is your Bible reading plan?

Feel free to change up your plan. Read the same chapter for five straight days. Do a word study. Listen to the Word while you walk or drive. Draw while you read the Bible. Enjoy God's Word.

SOWERS KNEEDED: DEVOTION 3

MYSTERY MAN

Dr. Randy T. Johnson | Growth Pastor

I may not be the sharpest spoon in the drawer, yet I do know there are things I will not know. There are things in life we will not understand. If I had been the "creator," we would have been in trouble. The story would have gone something like, "On the sixth day man and woman were created. On the sixth night, they went to sleep, and all of their muscles relaxed, so they died." Seriously, is it not amazing how God created us? He did not miss a detail from the number of hairs on our head to our very fingerprints. We are fearfully and wonderfully made.

In Mark 4:26-29 Jesus gives another parable on the seed being scattered:

"And he said, 'The kingdom of God is as if a man should scatter seed on the ground. He sleeps and rises night and day, and the seed sprouts and grows; he knows not how. The earth produces by itself, first the blade, then the ear, then the full grain in the ear. But when the grain is ripe, at once he puts in the sickle, because the harvest has come.'"

Seeds sprout and grow, and we cannot even comprehend it. How did something come from basically nothing? A seed can grow to a myriad of its original size even producing hundreds of more seeds.

I think the parable describes another mystery – true salvation. It is such a treat to see lives changed by Jesus Christ. Possessions, drugs, power, friends, and even self can consume someone until they meet Jesus. Lives can be changed. 2 Corinthians 5:17 says, **"Therefore, if anyone is in Christ, he is a new creation. The old has passed away; behold, the new has come."** You have

God in you giving you the power, guidance, and motivation to walk in truth. You wake up each morning with purpose. God has a plan for the day and your life.

Salvation makes us a new creation. We can and must grow. Healthy beings produce fruit. Obviously, the Holy Spirit makes repentance possible. It is such a mystery how that can happen. We are saved by faith, not works. We are sanctified (grow) by faith, not works.

You are new in Christ. Shine!

Walk with confidence. Step up and out!

SOWERS KNEEDED: DEVOTION 4

ABBA, FATHER

Dr. Randy T. Johnson | Growth Pastor

There are no grandchildren in Heaven, only children. Each person has to make a decision concerning Jesus Christ on his or her own. No one else can make it for them. No one can get into Heaven on someone else's prayer, giving, reputation, or standing. We must personally become a child of God.

This thought sunk in while reading Mark 4:26-29:

"And he said, 'The kingdom of God is as if a man should scatter seed on the ground. He sleeps and rises night and day, and the seed sprouts and grows; he knows not how. The earth produces by itself, first the blade, then the ear, then the full grain in the ear. But when the grain is ripe, at once he puts in the sickle, because the harvest has come.'"

The sower planted the seed and then waited. There is nothing he can do. This can be true in raising children, too. Proverbs 22:6 is a principle, *"Train up a child in the way he should go; even when he is old he will not depart from it."* We need to raise the next generation in such a way that they see the need for God. They need to feel the void and seek for truth. They need to turn their life to God.

There are three words that can guide our parenting. First is patience. The sower knew he had to wait. It reminds me of God waiting for the prodigal son to return. They do not always return, but when they do arms are open wide.

Second is prayer. The parable does not say prayer, but I remember living in Cadillac and knew the farmers were praying and asking for prayer. Flooding and drought were both concerns. Having too much or too little can be tough on our kids. We need to pray.

The third is perseverance. Galatians 6:9 says, **"And let us not grow weary of doing good, for in due season we will reap, if we do not give up."** The farmer must press on. He cannot give up. We must continue to be an example and to spread the love. Stay active and focused on the Lord. Parenting is not easy, but it is worth it.

I was shocked when I first saw 1 Samuel 8:5: **"Behold, you are old and your sons do not walk in your ways. Now appoint for us a king to judge us like all the nations."** The great man of God raised sons that changed the course of time. His sons were so bad that Israel switched from judges to a king. We will not be perfect as parents, but even the godly ones have their battles. The child has to make Jesus his own personal savior.

David was "a man after God's own heart." Yet, David's life with his kids would make an outrageous reality show: One son rapes his sister. A son kills his brother. One son even tries to kill David. It has a sad story line until we reach his distant relative – Jesus.

One of my favorite verses is 3 John 1:4: **"I have no greater joy than to hear that my children are walking in the truth."** I felt this as a teacher and definitely as a parent. My wife and I even have this verse framed in our living room. It is a reminder to our children and us.

Parents – patience, prayer, and perseverance are key.

There are only children in Heaven.

SOWERS KNEEDED: DEVOTION 5

AN OFFSHOOT

Dr. Randy T. Johnson | Growth Pastor

What is Deoxyribonucleic Acid? It appears for about $100 you can buy a kit that helps you find out your ethnicity and possibly family heritage. All they need is a little saliva. This "spit" contains your DNA. Your DNA reveals a lot about yourself.

An interesting name for Jesus is "Branch." At first glance, the name Branch seems pretty basic or simple; however, it is rich is meaning. It implies Jesus' DNA. Jesus is the offshoot of David's line. Jesus fulfilled all the prophecy for the Messiah!

Isaiah 11:1 says, *"There shall come forth a shoot from the stump of Jesse, and a branch from his roots shall bear fruit."* Jeremiah 23:5 continues the thought, *"Behold, the days are coming, declares the Lord, when I will raise up for David a righteous Branch, and he shall reign as king and deal wisely, and shall execute justice and righteousness in the land."* Twice Zechariah refers to the Branch:

"Hear now, O Joshua the high priest, you and your friends who sit before you, for they are men who are a sign: behold, I will bring my servant the Branch" (3:8).

"And say to him, 'Thus says the Lord of hosts, 'Behold, the man whose name is the Branch: for he shall branch out from his place, and he shall build the temple of the Lord'" (6:12).

Revelation 5:5 speaks of the future and adds another name (and prophecy) for Jesus:

"And one of the elders said to me, 'Weep no more; behold, the Lion of the tribe of Judah, the Root of David, has conquered, so that he can open the scroll and its seven seals.'"

There are even more passages that talk about the Messiah coming from David. Prophecy required the Messiah to originate from the line of David. He needed David's DNA. It is important.

Josh McDowell records that are some 330 prophecies concerning the Messiah that are all fulfilled in Jesus. He mentions that Victory Publishing House is willing to give $1000 to anyone who can find even 40 of the prophecies fulfilled in any other person. Jesus 330, everyone else gets less than 40. That is amazing!

John 15 goes even further in mentioning that believers are "little branches." As a child of God, we have Jesus' DNA.

Deoxyribonucleic Acid (DNA) is changing the way we think. It has even reversed some long-standing court cases. DNA tells a story.

We are an offshoot of Jesus. A branch that is fruitful will be pruned, but an unfruitful branch will be cut off and destroyed. When difficulties come, remember Jesus might be molding us.

Enjoy being part of the family.

Walk in a way that honors your family heritage.

SOWERS KNEEDED: DEVOTION 6

TRINITY

Dr. Randy T. Johnson | Growth Pastor

I do not spend much time on infomercials. It takes thirty minutes for them to show us the next best thing. And if I call in the next five minutes they will double or even triple the value. I have thought about calling in and saying, "I realize it has been eight minutes and that I did not call in the first five minutes so I only get one super-duper item I cannot live without. Bummer." Then hang up. By the way, how much of a variance can there be in the word "handling" in shipping and handling?

In thinking of this next name of God it is as if an infomercial was really good for EVERYONE.

Who created the Heavens and Earth? The simple answer is God.

Genesis 1:1 says, ***"In the beginning, God created the heavens and the earth."*** It seems pretty obvious.

Colossians 1:16 appears to add a twist to this simple topic as it describes Jesus: ***"For by him all things were created, in heaven and on earth, visible and invisible, whether thrones or dominions or rulers or authorities—all things were created through him and for him."*** All things were created by Jesus.

In Job 33:4 Job says, ***"The Spirit of God has made me, and the breath of the Almighty gives me life."*** The Holy Spirit is referenced as the Creator.

So is God, Jesus, or the Holy Spirit the Creator? Yes!

Genesis 1:1 uses the word "Elohim" for God. It is the second most common name for God in the Bible. A lot of people would recognize that "El" stands for God. The "ohim" in Hebrew is equivalent to the "s" we use to pluralize a word in the English language.

Elohim brings out God as the All-Powerful One. He is the Creator. He is God the Father, God the Son, and God the Holy Spirit.

In Genesis 1:26 the word Elohim is used again. It is interesting to see the pronoun use of this verse: ***"Then God said, 'Let us make man in our image, after our likeness. And let them have dominion over the fish of the sea and over the birds of the heavens and over the livestock and over all the earth and over every creeping thing that creeps on the earth.'"*** God uses the pronoun "our" twice. It is ***"our image"*** and ***"our likeness."*** Again the concept of the Trinity working in perfect harmony is displayed.

Deuteronomy 10:17 draws out the picture of God as Elohim in saying, ***"For the Lord your God is God of gods and Lord of lords, the great, the mighty, and the awesome God, who is not partial and takes no bribe."*** God is all-powerful, but when you change it to a three in one package, you have tripled the emphasis. He is even three times greater and stronger than initially thought of in the simple word God.

Walk with confidence claiming Romans 8:31: ***"What then shall we say to these things? If God is for us, who can be against us?"***

It is even better than you thought. You get a three in one deal with no cost in shipping and handling.

5

KINGDOM CHAT

Dr. Randy T. Johnson | Growth Pastor

In this lesson we will cover three parables: the Weeds (Tares) and Wheat, the Net (Dragnet), and the Sheep and Goats. It is interesting to note the use of different words and phrases: the Kingdom of God, the Kingdom of Heaven, Heaven, Kingdom, and Eternal Life.

1. Matthew 13 talks about weeds (tares) that look like wheat for a while.

Matthew 13:24-30
"He put another parable before them, saying, "The kingdom of heaven may be compared to a man who sowed good seed in his field, but while his men were sleeping, his enemy came and sowed weeds among the wheat and went away. So when the plants came up and bore grain, then the weeds appeared also. And the servants of the master of the house came and said to him, 'Master, did you not sow good seed in your field? How then does it have weeds?' He said to them, 'An enemy has done this.' So the servants said to him, 'Then do you want us to go and gather them?' But he said, 'No, lest in gathering the weeds you root up the wheat along with them. Let both grow together until the harvest, and

at harvest time I will tell the reapers, Gather the weeds first and bind them in bundles to be burned, but gather the wheat into my barn.'"

Do you like to garden? If so, describe what you do. _____
_____
_____
_____

Who is the enemy? What are his "weeds"? _____
Satan - doubt, lies, anger

Wheat has fruit/nut to it; weeds are empty. How does this apply?
Weeds look good but they have no substanaha

Matthew 13:36-43

"Then he left the crowds and went into the house. And his disciples came to him, saying, 'Explain to us the parable of the weeds of the field.' He answered, 'The one who sows the good seed is the Son of Man. The field is the world, and the good seed is the sons of the kingdom. The weeds are the sons of the evil one, and the enemy who sowed them is the devil. The harvest is the end of the age, and the reapers are angels. Just as the weeds are gathered and burned with fire, so will it be at the end of the age. The Son of Man will send his angels, and they will gather out of his kingdom all causes of sin and all law-breakers, and throw them into the fiery furnace. In that place there will be weeping and gnashing of teeth. Then the righteous will shine like the

sun in the kingdom of their Father. He who has ears, let him hear.'"

Who is the enemy? What are his "weeds"? _____
_____
_____
_____

Describe the two end destinies. _____
_____
_____

2. Matthew 13 continues with the parable of a fishing net (Dragnet).

Matthew 13:47-50

"Again, the kingdom of heaven is like a net that was thrown into the sea and gathered fish of every kind. When it was full, men drew it ashore and sat down and sorted the good into containers but threw away the bad. So it will be at the end of the age. The angels will come out and separate the evil from the righteous and throw them into the fiery furnace. In that place there will be weeping and gnashing of teeth."

Could the Jews eat fish of every kind? _____
_____
_____

Is Heaven, Hell, or both described here? _____
_____
_____
_____

Does this passage allow for the belief that everyone will end up in Heaven? _____
_____
_____

3. In Matthew 25 Jesus uses Sheep and Goats in His parable.

Matthew 25:31-40

"When the Son of Man comes in his glory, and all the angels with him, then he will sit on his glorious throne. Before him will be gathered all the nations, and he will separate people one from another as a shepherd separates the sheep from the goats. And he will place the sheep on his right, but the goats on the left. Then the King will say to those on his right, 'Come, you who are blessed by my Father, inherit the kingdom prepared for you from the foundation of the world. For I was hungry and you gave me food, I was thirsty and you gave me drink, I was a stranger and you welcomed me, I was naked and you clothed me, I was sick and you visited me, I was in prison and you came to me.' Then the righteous will answer him, saying, 'Lord, when did we see you hungry and feed you, or thirsty and give you drink? And when did we see you a stranger and welcome you, or naked and clothe you? And when did we see you sick or in prison and visit you?' And the King will answer them, 'Truly, I say to you, as you did it to one of the least of these my brothers, you did it to me.'"

What is the time frame of this parable? _____
_____
_____

Who are the sheep? Is this a common description for them?
_____
_____
_____

Who are the goats? _____
_____
_____

Put verse 40 in your own words. _____
_____
_____
_____

Matthew 25:41-46

"Then he will say to those on his left, 'Depart from me, you cursed, into the eternal fire prepared for the devil and his angels. For I was hungry and you gave me no food, I was thirsty and you gave me no drink, I was a stranger and you did not welcome me, naked and you did not clothe me, sick and in prison and you did not visit me.' Then they also will answer, saying, 'Lord, when did we see you hungry or thirsty or a stranger or naked or sick or in prison, and did not minister to you?' Then he will answer them, saying, 'Truly, I say to you, as you did not do it to one of the least of these, you did not do it to me.' And these will go away into eternal punishment, but the righteous into eternal life."

How does this passage compare to James 2? _____
_____
_____
_____

Why did Jesus use the phrase *"least of these"*? _____
_____
_____
_____

When were you in need and someone reached out? _____
_____
_____
_____

Who are the *"least of these"* around us each day? _____
_____
_____
_____

Pray to have the eyes of Jesus to see others as He does and then look into the eyes of strangers and search for Jesus.

KINGDOM KHAT: DEVOTION 1

POKEMON GO... INTO ALL THE WORLD

Dr. Randy T. Johnson | Growth Pastor

Do you remember the craze of Pokemon Go last summer? Nintendo's stock went crazy until it was revealed that Nintendo did not develop Pokemon Go. The stock took major hits. I wonder how many people went crazy buying stock just to lose it all in about ten days. It is sad, but when you believe in something you should go all out. I wondered how many Nintendo workers sold their stock at its peak knowing they did not develop it.

The movie, *Back to the Future*, brought up a lot of ideas. It made people wonder where they would go, whom they would visit, and what they would do if they could travel time. One of the common themes was how you could have changed your finances. What would someone do if they knew they could go back and invest in Nike or Apple? How much gold would you buy?

Matthew 13:45-46 kind of gives this scenario, *"Again, the kingdom of heaven is like a merchant in search of fine pearls, who, on finding one pearl of great value, went and sold all that he had and bought it."*

This merchant goes to check out some garage sales. He finds the one steal of a lifetime. He does not have enough money, but he knows it will top the charts. He sells his fishing gear, golf clubs, tools, lawn mower, motorcycle, car, and even house. He sells it all just to buy this one pearl. He is all in.

The question that begs for an answer, "How much do you believe Heaven is real?" Maybe a more painful question would be, "how much do you believe Hell is for real?"

When you believe in something, you should go all out. You should be all in!

Jesus said, ***"Go therefore and make disciples of all nations, baptizing them in the name of the Father and of the Son and of the Holy Spirit, teaching them to observe all that I have commanded you. And behold, I am with you always, to the end of the age"*** (Matthew 28:19-20).

Jesus said that we need to go and make a difference in the world. He is not sending us alone into the unknown; He is going with us.

Are you spending too much time and finances on a hobby? Does it own you?

I am not saying to sell it. Ask God how it can be used to help others find the Kingdom of God.

KINGDOM KHAT: DEVOTION 2

BEANS, RICE, AND JESUS CHRIST

Dr. Randy T. Johnson | Growth Pastor

I have been to Mexico many times. I am not sure what image Mexico conveys for you, but my first fifteen times I took high school students to some very remote places. Initially, we would take on a building project and play soccer with the local talent as a way to develop rapport. After sharing the Gospel, we would give food, clothing, and medical supplies. We were constantly in villages with no electricity or running water. One of the days we would go to "the garbage dump." I remember as a child going up north camping when at dusk we would go to the local dump to watch the bear come out (it does not seem as bright or exciting now). In Mexico, I was left with a different feeling.

It was November of 1995 when I first took a group to Mexico and eventually "the garbage dump." I had already preached with an interpreter and was handing out bottles of orange drink. When I gave out the last bottle, I stood there confounded. I did not know what to do with the box. My thought was, "Is it okay to litter in a garbage dump?" That may not sound like a difficult question, but I did not know what to do. A local missionary asked me, "What are you going to do?" I guess my blank stare answered his question as he said, "These men would like the box. It will be used as part of a wall for their house." I do not know if big boys are allowed to cry, but my allergies sure did flare up.

Reading Matthew 25 takes me back to Mexico when I read,

"Then the King will say to those on his right, 'Come, you who are blessed by my Father, inherit the kingdom prepared for you from the foundation of the world. For I was hungry, and you gave me food, I was thirsty and you gave me drink, I

was a stranger and you welcomed me, I was naked and you clothed me, I was sick and you visited me, I was in prison and you came to me.' Then the righteous will answer him, saying, 'Lord, when did we see you hungry and feed you, or thirsty and give you drink? And when did we see you a stranger and welcome you, or naked and clothe you? And when did we see you sick or in prison and visit you?' And the King will answer them, 'Truly, I say to you, as you did it to one of the least of these my brothers, you did it to me'" (verses 34-40).

I have been to Cancun. I have been spoiled at a resort. It was restful and even helpful. I was glad I went, but I could not wait to come back home. "The garbage dump" was different. Part of my heart stayed in Matamoros, Mexico. I went there to be a blessing. I wanted to experience, **"as you did it to one of the least of these my brothers, you did it to me."** In the process I was blessed. I was changed. I know the world may view these brothers and sisters as **"the least."** As they have recognized me returning on numerous trips, they greet and encourage me. Maybe, at that moment I am one of **"the least."**

Who is someone you can help today that has no apparent one of repaying you?

Do it for Jesus – literally!

KINGDOM KHAT: DEVOTION 3

"A JOURNEY BACK"

Dr. Randy T. Johnson | Growth Pastor

In 2016 I wrote a book with a close friend entitled, *A Journey Back*. It was his story on how God used three years in prison to get his attention and bring him back to the fold. I wrote him regularly and visited a few times. His family stuck with him, but several friends disowned him. He told me that he would read my letters to his cellblock because most inmates do not get any mail.

Upon writing the book, we contacted a few agents and publishers. They were not interested because it was not financial suitable for them. Prisoners cannot afford books. They do not have anything we need. So why would anyone care about them? Maybe we should care about them because Jesus does.

Matthew 25:35-36 says, **"For I was hungry and you gave me food, I was thirsty and you gave me drink, I was a stranger and you welcomed me, I was naked and you clothed me, I was sick and you visited me, I was in prison and you came to me."**

Jesus specifically mentions prisons. When was Jesus in prison? The only recorded times in Scripture are the night before the crucifixion. When He is speaking with them, He has not experienced inmate life yet. They ask Him when all of this happened. He clarifies in verse 40 by saying, **"And the King will answer them, 'Truly, I say to you, as you did it to one of the least of these my brothers, you did it to me.'"**

By visiting inmates or anyone in need, we visit Jesus. Encouraging them encourages Jesus! I have been encouraged to see so many friends receive training so they can visit inmates. It is costly. Often they have to take time off work, drive a few hundred miles, and even pay for a hotel room. Others could not go so they helped support those going and have bought thousands of copies of the book to give to inmates. People are giving to those in need. God is smiling.

We need to reach out to people that are forgotten.

They need hope. They need love.

They need Jesus.

KINGDOM KHAT: DEVOTION 4

WHERE'S THE NEXT DANCE

Dr. Randy T. Johnson | Growth Pastor

Several years ago I was sitting down at a table to eat lunch and I bowed my head to pray. One guy teased that I must have partied too hard the night before because I was falling asleep at lunch. Another guy corrected him letting them know I was praying to thank God and ask Him to bless my food (Sorry, I did hear them while I was praying). When I looked back up to eat, the one guy swore about the food and said I better pray for all of them. So I did. It was an easy transition to ask what they believed about God. Interesting answers. When I asked if they believed in Heaven and Hell and what had to be done to know where they were going, one guy's answer has bothered me for years. He said, "I do not care where I go, I have friends in both places." He then went on to mock that he will party wherever he ends up.

In Luke 16 Jesus gives a parable about two men, a rich man, and a poor man. The rich man's problem is not his money, but his heart and he ends up in Hades. The poor man was carried to Abraham's side. From the "party" in Hades we learn, ***"And in Hades, being in torment, he lifted up his eyes and saw Abraham far off and Lazarus at his side. And he called out, 'Father Abraham, have mercy on me, and send Lazarus to dip the end of his finger in water and cool my tongue, for I am in anguish in this flame'"*** (verses 23-24). Words like torment, anguish, and flames are not comforting. A prideful man begging for mercy with no remorse or hope is sad.

Hell is real. I do not want anyone to go to Hell. I do not feel by being a Christian that I am better than anyone else. I am passionate about people knowing the truth. It may be more important to know what we are saved from rather than what we are saved to. Even God does not want people to go to Hell. 2 Peter 3:9 says, ***"The Lord is not slow to fulfill his promise as some count slowness, but is patient toward you, not wishing that any should perish, but that all should reach repentance."***

There is not a party in Hell. There is anguish. Verses 27-28 find the rich man worried about his family, ***"And he said, 'Then I beg you, father, to send him to my father's house—for I have five brothers—so that he may warn them, lest they also come into this place of torment.'"***

Hell is real. As long as we have breath, we can proclaim the name of Christ. But once we die, decision time is over – forever. We cannot change our own destiny or anyone else's.

Please examine your own story.
Please check on your friends while you can.

The only party will be in Heaven.

KINGDOM KHAT: DEVOTION 5

HE STARTED START!

Dr. Randy T. Johnson | Growth Pastor

I like studying personalities. I remember LaHaye's categories. The Sanguine is full of energy, the life of the party, and typically a great storyteller. The Choleric is a natural leader who tends to take control. The Melancholy has transferred into the English language as sadness, but they tend to be precise, detailed, and focus on quality. Finally, the Phlegmatic is loyal, easy-going, and often a good listener.

Gary Smalley and John Trent explain the four in terms of animals. The Sanguine is pictured as the playful otter. The Choleric sports the king of the jungle in the lion. The Melancholy is hard working behind the scenes as a beaver. The Phlegmatic is as loyal as a Golden Retriever.

Something very basic is that Sanguine and Choleric individuals are good starters, but weak finishers. Melancholy and Phlegmatic people are the opposite. Starters will start a book or puzzle and do not care if they finish it. Not so with the finishers. It might take them a while to pick a book, but they feel they must finish it no matter how bad it is. It is beautiful; we need each other.

My mom was a counselor and use to say that Jesus had all the strengths of all four personality types. His title from Hebrews 12:1-2 conveys this point, *"Therefore, since we are surrounded by so great a cloud of witnesses, let us also lay aside every weight, and sin which clings so closely, and let us run with endurance the race that is set before us, looking to Jesus, the founder and perfecter of our faith, who for the joy that was set before him endured the cross, despising the shame, and is seated at the right hand of the throne of God."*

Jesus is the Founder and Perfecter. He is the Author and Finisher.

The Book of Revelation describes the same concept with different titles.

"'I am the Alpha and the Omega,' says the Lord God, 'who is and who was and who is to come, the Almighty'" (1:8).

"And he said to me, 'It is done! I am the Alpha and the Omega, the beginning and the end. To the thirsty I will give from the spring of the water of life without payment'" (21:6).

"I am the Alpha and the Omega, the first and the last, the beginning and the end" (22:13).

Jesus is the Alpha and Omega, the First and the Last, and the Beginning and the End.

I like to think of it this way:
Jesus did not begin when the beginning began; He began the beginning. He did not start when start got started; He started start.

Be encouraged by Philippians 1:6, **"And I am sure of this, that he who began a good work in you will bring it to completion at the day of Jesus Christ."** Jesus is working in you, and He is not finished yet.

KINGDOM KHAT: DEVOTION 6

PRIEST AND KING

Dr. Randy T. Johnson | Growth Pastor

Who was both a priest and a king in the Bible? Yes, Jesus is the natural answer, but who else?

The First Amendment was written to protect the church from the government, not vice versa. It says, "Congress shall make no law respecting an establishment of religion, or prohibiting the free exercise thereof; or abridging the freedom of speech, or of the press; or the right of the people peaceably to assemble, and to petition the government for a redress of grievances." There is so much talk of separation and state. In the Bible, there is a man who leads both campaigns. His name is Melchizedek. He was a priest and king.

Genesis 14:17-22 says,
"After his return from the defeat of Chedorlaomer and the kings who were with him, the king of Sodom went out to meet him at the Valley of Shaveh (that is, the King's Valley). And Melchizedek king of Salem brought out bread and wine. (He was a priest of God Most High.) And he blessed him and said, 'Blessed be Abram by God Most High, Possessor of heaven and earth; and blessed be God Most High, who has delivered your enemies into your hand!' And Abram gave him a tenth of everything. And the king of Sodom said to Abram, 'Give me the persons, but take the goods for yourself.' But Abram said to the king of Sodom, 'I have lifted my hand to the Lord, God Most High, Possessor of heaven and earth.'"

My goal is not to talk politics; it is to see what name this priest and king used for God. It is El Elyon and means "The God Most High." It is used four times in this passage. This God Most High blesses people. There is not anything better than being blessed by God!

Daniel 4:34 reverses the blessing, ***"At the end of the days I, Nebuchadnezzar, lifted my eyes to heaven, and my reason returned to me, and I blessed the Most High, and praised and honored him who lives forever, for his dominion is an everlasting dominion, and his kingdom endures from generation to generation."*** Daniel blesses God. We should bless God. We should be a blessing to God.

Psalm 78:35 comforts His people in saying, ***"They remembered that God was their rock, the Most High God their redeemer."*** The God Most High is our foundation. He is our Redeemer.

I am more interested in being biblically correct than politically correct. I do not want to follow a political party; I want to follow Christ. The world does not need more or even better government; the world needs Jesus. Through Jesus, we have access to the Most High God!

6

STANDING SMALL

Dr. Randy T. Johnson | Growth Pastor

On February 1, 1986 I was living in Dallas, Texas. I was offered tickets to Reunion Arena for the NBA Slam Dunk Contest. Dominique Wilkins was the clear favorite and not much more was expected to happen. It was the day before our son's first birthday, so I decided to pass.

History was made. It is still one of the most influential dunk tournaments of all time. Dominique was impressive, but a guy thirteen inches shorter than him stole the show. Five foot 7 inch (some say that is generous) Anthony Jerome Webb jumped out of the gym. The 10-foot rim was no real challenge. "Spud" went on to win the dunk contest. He even jumped in the air, spun all the way around, and then dunked the ball. It is called a 360-degree dunk. I could have been there.

Spud walked a little taller that night. People respected him. Even the secular announcers referred to it as a "David and Goliath" feat.

There are times when the smallest things get our attention. Those with allergies carefully read the ingredients label. A text on your phone can bring a myriad of emotions. The girlfriend who wants to take the relationship to the next level is hoping for a gift in a small box.

If you are married, describe your proposal or share one of the most creative one's you have ever heard. _____
_____
_____
_____

What is one of the best gifts you have ever given or received?
_____
_____
_____

Jesus uses two simple, yet small items to convey the power of small.

1. The Mustard Seed

I remember when I went to Israel and I was first given a Mustard Seed. I was excited until I looked at it. I was not impressed. It was round and much larger than I expected. The person who gave it to me set me up. He smiled and broke open the "pod" and at least one hundred "seeds" smaller that the period on this sentence poured out into my hand.

Matthew 13:31-32
"He put another parable before them, saying, 'The kingdom of heaven is like a grain of mustard seed that a man took and sowed in his field. It is the smallest of all seeds, but when it has grown it is larger than all the garden plants and becomes a tree, so that the birds of the air come and make nests in its branches.'"

What is the kingdom of heaven? _____
_____
_____

Is it important that the mustard seed was the smallest of all seeds? _____
_____
_____

What helps the "seed" grow? _____
_____
_____

Does this parable convey anything about the future? _____
_____
_____
_____

What are the other garden plants, birds, nests, and branches (not all aspects of a parable have significance)? _____
_____
_____
_____

2. Leaven

My wife and I like fruit. Bananas, blueberries, cherries, strawberries, cantaloupe, watermelon, raspberries, plums, grapes, clementines, and most kinds of apples make a great snack. My wife likes Mangos and Kiwi more than me. By the way, please don not add tomatoes to my fruit salad.

What fruit is Michigan known for? _____
_____
_____

Ever so often we will buy too many apples and one will go bad. It is amazing how fast the rest of the basket starts going bad. What do they say about one bad apple? _____
_____

Matthew 13:33

"He told them another parable. 'The kingdom of heaven is like leaven that a woman took and hid in three measures of flour, till it was all leavened.'"

What is leaven? _____
_____
_____

Did the Jews own leaven? Did they ever not use it? _____
_____
_____
_____

Is leaven bad? What is leaven in this parable? _____
_____
_____
_____

1 Corinthians 15:33

"Do not be deceived: 'Bad company ruins good morals.'"

What does this verse mean? _____
_____
_____

Does good company "ruin" bad morals? Should there be guidelines?
_____
_____
_____

How do we help "the leaven" influence the whole bowl? _____
_____
_____
_____

"I long to accomplish a great and noble task, but it is my chief duty to accomplish small tasks as if they were great and noble."
Helen Keller

STANDING SMALL: DEVOTION 1

PEANUTS

Dr. Randy T. Johnson | Growth Pastor

"I get paid peanuts." That is usually not intended as a positive statement. The history of the declaration is unsure, but peanuts have been around for a long time and have always been viewed as having little value. When flying, I have not heard much excitement about peanuts replacing a meal. Peanuts? Are not those for the zoo? Do we not snack on them at certain restaurants and throw the shells on the floor? Peanuts? Do they have any value?

George Washington Carver is one of my heroes. He did not give up on something based on outward appearance. He took the peanut to an incredible level. He created some 300 uses for the "valueless" peanut. He made things like peanut sausage, caramel, mayonnaise, coffee, shampoo, shaving cream, glue, rubber, and even nitroglycerine. That is the bomb!

In Matthew 13:31-32 Jesus talks about an apparently insignificant seed that rises above the rest, *"He put another parable before them, saying, 'The kingdom of heaven is like a grain of mustard seed that a man took and sowed in his field. It is the smallest of all seeds, but when it has grown it is larger than all the garden plants and becomes a tree, so that the birds of the air come and make nests in its branches.'"*

The mustard seed is as small as the smallest dot you can make with a pen. It is smaller than a grain of pepper. It looks like black dust that you would brush aside. It grows from a plant into a tree.

Jesus is talking about His following that will become the Kingdom of Heaven. They look unimpressive, but they end up shaking the world. They will reign forever.

We need to focus on helping the Kingdom of Heaven to grow. A starting point is to get past outward appearance. Look for potential. With God man has value, purpose, and meaning. Reach out to all. Make a difference. Help change the world. Do not be fooled by outward appearance; everyone needs Jesus.

Take a moment the next time you are at a restaurant that has peanuts on the table. As you snack on a few and throw the shells on the ground (that was so fun as a kid), remember Dr. Carver who filled a grocery list with them. Also, remember that outward appearance can be deceptive.

Everyone you see today has value (even the person in the mirror)!

STANDING SMALL: DEVOTION 2

INFLUENCER

Dr. Randy T. Johnson | Growth Pastor

Do you have any fun stories of your first times doing the laundry? Did you use too much detergent, so the bubbles overflowed? Did a whole load come out pink? Did you splash a little bleach on some jeans only to find out now that you were a trendsetter? Obviously, I saw these all in movies, as I would not have made such a mistake.

Generally, we spend a lot of time avoiding bad influences. We know that one rotten apple spoils the whole bunch. We quote 1 Corinthians 15:33 saying, *"Do not be deceived: 'Bad company ruins good morals.'"* We strive on being separate. Jesus talks about leaven, and our first thought is its effect and a negative feel.

However, I like leaven. I want baked goods and bread to rise. Look at Matthew 13:33 and see what He compares leaven to, *"He told them another parable. 'The kingdom of heaven is like leaven that a woman took and hid in three measures of flour, till it was all leavened.'"*

The Kingdom of Heaven is going to impact the world. It is like leaven. It will grow. It calls for influencers. The word "influence" is only used three times in the Bible and all three are in 2 Corinthians 10 where Paul talks about the *"area of influence"* God has given them and how they pray it will be enlarged.

We do not have a home generator. I imagine that most of you do not either. Therefore, you know the sinking feeling of no power. You start searching around the house for a flashlight that has a good battery in it. Finally, you light a candle. That simple candle lights the whole room. It is amazing the impact light can have on darkness.

Jesus' prayer in John 17:16-18 says, *"They are not of the world, just as I am not of the world. Sanctify them in the truth; your word is truth. As you sent me into the world, so I have sent them into the world."* We are to look different from the worldly lifestyle, but God calls us to go into the world. We are to be influencers.

Where is your area of influence?

Are you an influencer for the Lord?

It is amazing the impact light can have on darkness.

STANDING SMALL: DEVOTION 3

BUG ME - FOREVER!

Dr. Randy T. Johnson | Growth Pastor

Children are intelligent. They typically know what parent to ask and when to ask for something that they might not normally get. They do not ask mom for a treat before dinner; they ask dad. But if dad is not home, they keep bugging mom until she gives in a little. And of course, if both parents say no, they ask grandma. Have you ever said, "Okay, just stop bugging me?"

Luke 18:1-8 gives a beautiful illustration of persistence in prayer, *"And he told them a parable to the effect that they ought always to pray and not lose heart. He said, 'In a certain city there was a judge who neither feared God nor respected man. And there was a widow in that city who kept coming to him and saying, 'Give me justice against my adversary.' For a while he refused, but afterward he said to himself, 'Though I neither fear God nor respect man, yet because this widow keeps bothering me, I will give her justice, so that she will not beat me down by her continual coming.' And the Lord said, 'Hear what the unrighteous judge says. And will not God give justice to his elect, who cry to him day and night? Will he delay long over them? I tell you, he will give justice to them speedily. Nevertheless, when the Son of Man comes, will he find faith on earth?'"*

We do not like nagging. It drains us. We do not like a judge changing his mind over nagging, but it happens. Jesus is telling us to 'nag and beg' in prayer.

The Daily Bread recorded a story of George Muller. George was known as a man of prayer. Books record the miracles he experienced, but on a personal note, he prayed for the salvation of five of his friends. They all got saved, but check out the time frame: first one after many months, second and third after ten years, fourth one took 25 years, and finally the fifth one came right after George's funeral. He had prayed for that friend 52 years.

Persistence in prayer involves focus and dedication. I am sure George Muller was not looking for personal praise for praying so long. I am convinced he did not care that he did not see the fruit of one of his friends in his lifetime. I know he just wanted the friend to acknowledge Jesus as Lord before he died.

What prayer request have you repeated for several years?

What family members or friends are you praying for their salvation or their walk with the Lord?

What family members and friends should you add to your list?

STANDING SMALL: DEVOTION 4

212 DEGREES

Dr. Randy T. Johnson | Growth Pastor

One of my favorite quotes of all time is by Sam Parker, "At 211 degrees, water is hot. At 212 degrees, it boils. And with boiling water, comes steam. And with steam, you can power a train. Just one extra degree makes all the difference."

How often do we give up right before victory was coming? This can be true of prayer, too.

Luke 18:1-8 gives a beautiful illustration of persistence in prayer, *"And he told them a parable to the effect that they ought always to pray and not lose heart. He said, 'In a certain city there was a judge who neither feared God nor respected man. And there was a widow in that city who kept coming to him and saying, 'Give me justice against my adversary.' For a while he refused, but afterward he said to himself, 'Though I neither fear God nor respect man, yet because this widow keeps bothering me, I will give her justice, so that she will not beat me down by her continual coming.' And the Lord said, 'Hear what the unrighteous judge says. And will not God give justice to his elect, who cry to him day and night? Will he delay long over them? I tell you, he will give justice to them speedily. Nevertheless, when the Son of Man comes, will he find faith on earth?'"*

Legend has it that Winston Churchill had a sliding scale for speaking engagements. He was once asked what it would cost to speak 20 minutes. He responded something like 10,000 pounds. "Oh, we cannot afford that. How about 10 minutes?" Churchill said that would be 20,000 pounds. Baffled the inquirer asked him why. Churchill said I do not have to think to speak twenty minutes because eventually, I will make a point, but I have to think before I speak ten minutes. I found the story amusing, but I wondered what then his most famous speech cost, "Never, never, never give up."

That speech is so powerful. Do not quit. Press on. Move forward. Do not slip.

Paul said it this way in Galatians 6:9, **"And let us not grow weary of doing good, for in due season we will reap, if we do not give up."** Even Elijah felt the burden of doing the right thing and feeling like it did not make a difference. God told him he was not alone. He needed to continue to be faithful. We need to trust God and keep on keeping on.

When you read the Bible and feel like you cannot understand it or it does not relate, keep reading.

When you pray and feel no one is there, keep praying.

When you go to church and feel everyone is fake, keep going.

When trusting and obeying God does not make good business sense, keep trusting Him. Keep obeying Him.

212 degrees might move trains, but prayer moves mountains!

STANDING SMALL: DEVOTION 5

HOUSE OF BREAD

Dr. Randy T. Johnson | Growth Pastor

Does fruitcake have any actual fruit in it? I like a cherry nut bread, but not necessarily fruitcake. As a child, I remember people we called "fruitcake." It was not intended to be a compliment. I also like cinnamon raisin bread, marble, whole wheat, Italian, and basically any kind. My wife's philosophy is, "The heavier the bread, the healthier it is for you." I would have loved trying manna.

In John 6:32-35 Jesus compares Himself to manna, *"Jesus then said to them, 'Truly, truly, I say to you, it was not Moses who gave you the bread from heaven, but my Father gives you the true bread from heaven. For the bread of God is he who comes down from heaven and gives life to the world.' They said to him, 'Sir, give us this bread always.' Jesus said to them, 'I am the bread of life; whoever comes to me shall not hunger, and whoever believes in me shall never thirst.'"*

As manna gave daily nourishment and sustenance, Jesus gave spiritual nourishment and sustenance. Manna only lasted awhile; Jesus is forever. He is the Bread of Life!

While the Israelites were wandering in the wilderness, God sent bread from Heaven every day. They would gather as much as they wanted. There was always enough for the day. It would spoil if they held onto it for another day, except Friday. On Friday they were to gather twice as much, and it never spoiled. They saw a miracle every day and the second one on Saturday morning. God provided for them. Acting in faith gave them the opportunity to see miracles.

God then sent His Son to be born in Bethlehem, which means "House of Bread." Bethlehem became the house of the Bread of Life. Jesus is the Bread of Life.

Psalm 34:8 continues the thought, **"Oh, taste and see that the Lord is good! Blessed is the man who takes refuge in him!"** God is good, all the time. All the time, God is good.

I like how Max Lucado approaches the title, "Bread of Life? Jesus lived up to the title. But an unopened loaf does a person no good. Have you received the bread? Have you received God's forgiveness?"

Daily go to Jesus seeking wisdom and discernment. He is the Bread of Life. He wants to meet your needs. Seven days without the Bread of Life makes one weak.

STANDING SMALL: DEVOTION 6

MONOVISION

Dr. Randy T. Johnson | Growth Pastor

I use to have 20/15 vision. What most people saw at 15 feet, I could see from 20 feet. I appreciated it and did not think I took it for granted. Then I turned 40. At age 40 my arms seemed shorter. I started holding things farther away and then eventually could not reach far enough. A lot of you know what I mean. First, I got progressive glasses, mainly for reading purposes. Then the doctor asked me to try something crazy. He invited me to try Monovision.

Monovision has worked perfectly for me. I only wear one contact. I wear a contact in my left eye for reading. I leave it in day and night for a whole month. I do not wear a contact in my right eye. It allows me to see far away. I think it is an excellent illustration of sanctifying. I set one eye apart for reading.

Jehovah-Mekaddishkem means the Lord who Sanctifies. In Exodus 31:12-13 we read, *"And the Lord said to Moses, 'You are to speak to the people of Israel and say, 'Above all you shall keep my Sabbaths, for this is a sign between me and you throughout your generations, that you may know that I, the Lord, sanctify you.'"* God set Israel apart. They are His people. He guided them through many trials.

God sets us apart as the body of Christ. Paul was assigned to the Gentiles. In 1 Thessalonians 5:23-24 he said, *"Now may the God of peace himself sanctify you completely, and may your whole spirit and soul and body be kept blameless at the coming of our Lord Jesus Christ. He who calls you is faithful; he will surely do it."* God set us apart to do something special, but He also set us apart to be holy. 1 Peter 1:15-16 continues the thought, ***"But as he who called you is holy, you also be holy in all your conduct, since it is written, 'You shall be holy, for I am holy.'"***

Hebrews 13:12 tells us how we were set apart, ***"So Jesus also suffered outside the gate in order to sanctify the people through his own blood."*** The life, death, and life again of Jesus were designed to pull us out of the slippery slope to Hell. He set us aside, not to live like the world, but to be holy.

I like Monovision, but my daily goal is to have both eyes on Jesus.

If you are a follower of Christ, then you have been set apart for something special. Is there anything in your walk that needs to change? Be holy. Walk the walk for which you were set apart.

7

THE THRILL IS IN THE SEARCH

Dr. Randy T. Johnson | Growth Pastor

I was raised with sports. My favorite sport was whatever season we were in. I had posters of Paul Warfield, Wilt Chamberlain, and Reggie Jackson on my wall. My family was sports nuts, too. My dad lettered thirteen times in high school. He turned down the opportunity for pro baseball and pro football. We had our favorite Tigers. My dad liked Al Kaline, my mom Bill Freeman, my sister is a lefty and liked Mickey Lolich, and my favorite was Willie Horton. My free time was sports related.

Not all kids are the same. Some put on a superhero outfit and a towel or pillowcase as their cape. They grab a garbage can cover. They run around with their wrapping paper tube saving the world.

Then there are the kids who used their imagination in finding hidden treasure. They would have loved Geocache or Pokemon Go, but we did not have access to GPS coordinates and technology. We had cleverly made maps.

What games did you play as a child? _____
_____
_____

What are some advantages and disadvantages of these games?
_____
_____
_____

Jesus gives three parables that involve seeking a treasure of great value.

1. Hidden Treasure

Matthew 13:44
"The kingdom of heaven is like treasure hidden in a field, which a man found and covered up. Then in his joy he goes and sells all that he has and buys that field."

What is taught about the Kingdom of Heaven? _____
_____
_____
_____

What does it mean today to ***"sells all that he has and buys that field"***? _____
_____
_____

2. Pearl of Great Price

Matthew 13:45-46
"Again, the kingdom of heaven is like a merchant in search of fine pearls, who, on finding one pearl of great value, went and sold all that he had and bought it."

Selling everything has obvious financial ramifications, but what energy and emotions should be experienced? _____
_____
_____
_____

What do you collect? Is there the ultimate find you would love to have?_____
_____
_____

3. The Lost Sheep

Matthew 18:12-14
"What do you think? If a man has a hundred sheep, and one of them has gone astray, does he not leave the ninety-nine on the mountains and go in search of the one that went astray? And if he finds it, truly, I say to you, he rejoices over it more than over the ninety-nine that never went astray. So it is not the will of my Father who is in heaven that one of these little ones should perish."

What causes "a sheep" to go astray? _____
_____
_____

Have you had a time in your life when you went astray? If so, what brought you back? _____
_____
_____
_____

What responsibility do we have with those who wander? _____
_____
_____

What should be our approach in bringing back the wandering sheep? _____
_____

What does the word ***"perish"*** mean to you? _____
_____
_____

C.C. Miller brings a unique perspective on this lost wandering sheep.

> "Twas a sheep not a lamb that strayed away
> In the parable Jesus told,
> A grown-up sheep that strayed away
> From the ninety and nine in the fold.
>
> And why for the sheep should we seek
> And earnestly hope and pray?
> Because there is danger when sheep go wrong;
> They lead the lambs astray.
>
> Lambs will follow the sheep, you know,
> Wherever the sheep may stray.
> When sheep go wrong, it won't take long
> Til the lambs are as wrong as they.
>
> And so with the sheep we earnestly plead
> For the sake of the lambs today,
> For when sheep are lost, what a terrible cost
> The lambs will have to pay!"

THE THRILL IS IN THE SEARCH: DEVOTION 1

HIDE-N-SEEK

Dr. Randy T. Johnson | Growth Pastor

When my wife and I got married, I was still in Seminary, so we lived in an apartment for three years. The one-bedroom apartment was fine until our son was born. We needed more space. I finished my degree, and we took a pastorate in Cadillac. It was time to do house shopping.

The church was just outside of town. We first looked in town for houses, but on our tight budget, it was not looking good. Finally, we found a house about seven miles from the church. We had always lived in the city, so this would be an adjustment. There were no sidewalks. I had to learn about well water, salt, water softeners, septic fields, iron-out, and propane gas. The house was on Valley Forge Drive, which should have been a warning about the weather we were going to encounter (coming from Dallas we did not even have winter coats).

The house was beautiful. Our parents came to help us look around. It had an attached garage (that was something I never had growing up), full basement, master bathroom, and large kitchen. We loved it. We then had a Joseph and Mary incident. No one had our 17-month old son. "I thought he was with you" was the general consensus. We knew he did not go downstairs or outside as we had been careful with doors, but we could not find him. Finally, after which seemed far too long, my dad found him resting in a kitchen cupboard. The cupboard was designed for large pots and pans but was then turned into a fort by the grandpas. They carpeted it and put in a battery operated light. Our son had his ideal hideout.

In Matthew 18:12-14 Jesus tells the parable of one seemingly getting away, *"What do you think? If a man has a hundred sheep, and one of them has gone astray, does he not leave the ninety-nine on the mountains and go in search of the one that went astray? And if he finds it, truly, I say to you, he rejoices over it more than over the ninety-nine that never went astray. So it is not the will of my Father who is in heaven that one of these little ones should perish."*

This lost sheep was important to the shepherd. He is not talking just about a sheep. Most of us have experienced that empty feeling in your gut when you cannot find your dog or even more important your child. The search goes on.

When our child is lost in a mall, we panic, pray, seek help, search relentlessly, and never give up. We will do anything to find them. We want them safe and home.

What about our children who spiritually wander?
Do we pray?
Do we try to help?
Do we refuse to give up?

THE THRILL IS IN THE SEARCH: DEVOTION 2

PICK'N FOREVER

Dr. Randy T. Johnson | Growth Pastor

I like garage sales, flea markets, and watching American Pickers. I even visited the American Pickers store when I was in Nashville. I am always looking for something. The problem is, I do not know what it is. I am blessed; I do not "need" anything. Fortunately, I have learned to go through a morning of picking without spending any money. My wife often thinks it is a mourning of picking.

Jesus uses two parables to convey the value of the kingdom of heaven. He says they are like a hidden treasure and a pearl of great price. Matthew 13:44-46 says, *"The kingdom of heaven is like treasure hidden in a field, which a man found and covered up. Then in his joy he goes and sells all that he has and buys that field. Again, the kingdom of heaven is like a merchant in search of fine pearls, who, on finding one pearl of great value, went and sold all that he had and bought it."*

The one guy finds a great treasure while the other a great pearl. They were searching and found their big hit. It is fun watching someone who has found "a treasure" and how they try to be calm so they can bargain their way to a good deal. Not so with these guys. They go all in. They sell everything and buy it.

This reminds me of the rich man who comes asking Jesus what he must do to inherit eternal life. Matthew 19:21-22 records the interaction, *"Jesus said to him, 'If you would be perfect, go, sell what you possess and give to the poor, and you will have treasure in heaven; and come, follow me.' When the young man heard this he went away sorrowful, for he had great*

possessions." He was not willing to be all in. He could be the fulfillment of the parables. He found the treasure in Jesus Christ and chose to walk away. He found the find of a lifetime but felt it cost too much.

Matthew 16:26 cuts so deep, ***"For what will it profit a man if he gains the whole world and forfeits his soul? Or what shall a man give in return for his soul?"*** Wealth can whither. We have seen that bankruptcy is no respecter of person.

Did you remember seeing something you wanted at a garage sale and did not buy but wish you did? Your mind went back and forth. You haggled over dollars and maybe even cents before you walked away.

The Kingdom of Heaven is on the table. Do not pass by it.

THE THRILL IS IN THE SEARCH: DEVOTION 3

BLANK PENNY

Dr. Randy T. Johnson | Growth Pastor

A few years ago I was at the drive-through of a fast-food restaurant. I had ordered a soft drink. I gave them $1.10 and waited for the four cents in change. When I received the change, it consisted of three pennies and a "slug." I know this will sound cheap, but I contemplated asking for my penny. I refrained. However, please realize if I see a penny on the ground I will pick it up whether it is heads or tails. When I got home, I looked a little closer at the "slug."

I realized that the "slug" was something different. It was the same size, shape, and even had the ridge of a penny. I went on-line and found it was a blank penny which is called a blank planchet. It is worth $50. Now, I had a new dilemma. I always return money when the cashier makes a mistake and gives me too much change back. Do I need to go back to the fast-food joint?

In Luke 15:8-10 we read about a parable concerning coins, *"Or what woman, having ten silver coins, if she loses one coin, does not light a lamp and sweep the house and seek diligently until she finds it? And when she has found it, she calls together her friends and neighbors, saying, 'Rejoice with me, for I have found the coin that I had lost.' Just so, I tell you, there is joy before the angels of God over one sinner who repents."* Some people may view it as not being a big deal, but every coin was important to her.

The real message is that every person is important.

You may feel like a blank planchet that people pass around as if you have no value. You are treated as a mistake or misfit. Do not believe the lie.

Please read Psalm 139:13-14 very personally, *"For you formed my inward parts; you knitted me together in my mother's womb. I praise you, for I am fearfully and wonderfully made. Wonderful are your works; my soul knows it very well."* You are handmade by God. He does not make mistakes. Your life is worth something big.

The next time you feel "blank" with people passing you by as if you are faceless, remember you are priceless. You are worth dying for.

Jesus died for you.

THE THRILL IS IN THE SEARCH: DEVOTION 4

LOSE A FRIEND?

Dr. Randy T. Johnson | Growth Pastor

In 2015 the New York Daily News ran an article about Americans losing things. They recorded that the top ten things lost or misplaced were car keys, house keys, winter accessories, clothing, credit or debit card, wallet, watch or jewelry, cash, umbrella, and driver's license. I thought it was an interesting list, but believe people lose their temper or lose their mind more often. They went on to say that Americans lose an average of $5,591 over a lifetime.

I remember someone asking me, "Why is it that I tend to find the item in the last place I look?" Really? I know we check obvious places first, but I manage to locate the item in the last place I look because once I find it, I stop looking. But, I digress.

The article went on to say that 1 in 5 people say they lose or misplace an item each week. Therefore, Jesus' parable of the lost coin in Luke 15:8-10 makes a lot of sense to us, ***"Or what woman, having ten silver coins, if she loses one coin, does not light a lamp and sweep the house and seek diligently until she finds it? And when she has found it, she calls together her friends and neighbors, saying, 'Rejoice with me, for I have found the coin that I had lost.' Just so, I tell you, there is joy before the angels of God over one sinner who repents."***

Losing something can be very frustrating. It often happens when we are in a hurry and need it now. We frantically run through the house asking, "Where are my keys?" It does not help when people ask, "Did you check your pockets, purse, or the car?" "Where was the last place you had them?"

Whatever the case, the woman in the parable, finds the coin and rejoices. She is thrilled and relieved. Jesus immediately tells us the meaning of the parable. Angels party when people get saved!

Scripture does not record angels rejoicing with a job promotion or someone getting approved for a home mortgage. Those are important, but angels rejoice over salvation.

What does your prayer request list look like?

Are you daily praying for the salvation of family and friends?

Lost keys, phone, and winter gloves can be replaced. Make sure you do not lose a friend – forever.

THE THRILL IS IN THE SEARCH: DEVOTION 5

REDEEMER

Dr. Randy T. Johnson | Growth Pastor

I have seen in the news times where people are stealing dogs for the hopeful cash reward that may come later or to even ransom them. Dog ransom? They are ransoming some kid's dog for a few thousand dollars. Twice I saw it with the Maltese breed. We had a Maltese. We called her "Lucy" for short. If someone stole her, they would have paid us to take her back. She seemed more like a cat than man's best friend. By the way, how did we get the term "cat burglar"? No one is stealing cats and holding them for ransom. Cats just end up on your porch from who knows where. As silly as dog ransom might sound, there was a ransom that affected all of us.

Mark 10:45 says, *"For even the Son of Man came not to be served but to serve, and to give his life as a ransom for many."* 1 Timothy 2:6 repeats the concept, *"Who gave himself as a ransom for all, which is the testimony given at the proper time."* We were held hostage by our sin. We were hell-bound when Jesus stepped in and paid a price we could not afford. He gave His perfect life up for us as a sacrifice and a ransom to redeem us.

Jesus is The Redeemer. His death is the payment for the ransom. Job 19:25 says, *"For I know that my Redeemer lives, and at the last he will stand upon the earth."* Reading this puts a song in my mind and my heart. I know my Redeemer lives. Although he paid the ransom with His life, He came back to life. He arose! My Redeemer lives!

The Book of Ruth is a historically accurate story that also gives a picture of a Kinsman Redeemer when Boaz rescues Ruth, *"So*

Boaz took Ruth, and she became his wife. And he went in to her, and the Lord gave her conception, and she bore a son. Then the women said to Naomi, 'Blessed be the Lord, who has not left you this day without a redeemer, and may his name be renowned in Israel!'" (4:13-14). Just as Boaz redeemed Ruth, Jesus offers redemption for us.

Romans 8:2 tells the story, ***"For the law of the Spirit of life has set you free in Christ Jesus from the law of sin and death."***

In most cases if people treated others as well as they treat their dog, the world would be a much brighter place. Please thank Jesus for His redeeming work in ransoming us by doing something special for Him through someone else today.

THE THRILL IS IN THE SEARCH: DEVOTION 6

THE PROVIDER

Dr. Randy T. Johnson | Growth Pastor

There are Bible stories that would have been great to stand off to the side and watch live. Most would say David against Goliath. The walls of Jericho dropping would have left one awestruck. Gideon and his "band" of 300 downing 125,000 would have left one speechless. I would have wanted to witness the selection process and Gideon's face. However, one that has drama, humor, and victory is the story of Abraham and Isaac.

Abraham was told to take his son, Isaac, and sacrifice him. He has his son on the altar showing full faith and obedience when God stops him. Genesis 22:13-14 picks up the story, *"And Abraham lifted up his eyes and looked, and behold, behind him was a ram, caught in a thicket by his horns. And Abraham went and took the ram and offered it up as a burnt offering instead of his son. So Abraham called the name of that place, 'The Lord will provide'; as it is said to this day, 'On the mount of the Lord it shall be provided.'"* Now, I have heard of firemen be called to rescue a cat from a tree, but I have never heard of a ram caught in a thicket. The timing is incredible. Abraham and Isaac are getting everything ready, and they do not even notice it, but it is waiting for God's perfect timing.

A title for God from this passage is Jehovah-Jireh, which means "The Lord Will Provide." Abraham realized the ram was from God. God provided in his deepest time.

Psalm 23:1 conveys the same concept, *"The Lord is my shepherd; I shall not want."* God will provide. David watched it as he shepherded his flock. He knew what it meant to be a shepherd and to provide.

Abraham saw God provide a son when he was 100 years old. He walked in faith and obedience. Even when it did not seem to make sense, he was faithful. He watched God provide again.

Hebrews 11:17-19 shares what Abraham was thinking, ***"By faith Abraham, when he was tested, offered up Isaac, and he who had received the promises was in the act of offering up his only son, of whom it was said, 'Through Isaac shall your offspring be named.' He considered that God was able even to raise him from the dead, from which, figuratively speaking, he did receive him back."***

He trusted God. He knew and experienced Jehovah-Jireh.

Where do you need to trust God? Is it a relationship? Finances? Time?

Look around, and you might see a ram in the thicket. Jehovah-Jireh is seeking to bless those who walk in faith.

8

FORGIVE GOD?

Dr. Randy T. Johnson | Growth Pastor

"Holding onto anger is like drinking poison and expecting the other person to die." This is a famous quote with no real origin. It has been modified and used in many sources. The only antidote is forgiveness.

Why do we struggle with forgiving others? _____
_____
_____
_____

What are several reasons why we should forgive someone?
_____
_____
_____

Who is the hardest person to forgive: God, family, friends, others, or self? _____
_____
_____

Matthew 18:23-35 contains the parable of The Unforgiving Servant.

23 "Therefore the kingdom of heaven may be compared to a king who wished to settle accounts with his servants."

Who would you guess is the king and who are his servants?

_____
_____
_____

24 "When he began to settle, one was brought to him who owed him ten thousand talents. 25 And since he could not pay, his master ordered him to be sold, with his wife and children and all that he had, and payment to be made."

Ten thousand talents were equivalent to millions of dollars.

Was the king being fair? _____
_____
_____

How could someone build up such a debt? _____
_____
_____
_____

26 "So the servant fell on his knees, imploring him, 'Have patience with me, and I will pay you everything.' 27 And out of pity for him, the master of that servant released him and forgave him the debt."

Do you think the servant could eventually repay him? _____
_____
_____
_____

How does the word 'pity' affect you? _____
_____
_____

28 "But when that same servant went out, he found one of his fellow servants who owed him a hundred denarii, and seizing him, he began to choke him, saying, 'Pay what you owe.'"

(A denarius was equivalent to a day's wages. Matthew 20:1-2 says, **"For the kingdom of heaven is like a master of a house who went out early in the morning to hire laborers for his vineyard. After agreeing with the laborers for a denarius a day, he sent them into his vineyard."**)

What was the difference in the amount owed by the two men?
_____
_____
_____

Do you think this man could eventually have paid back his debt?
_____
_____
_____

Why was the man so mad? _____
_____
_____

29 "So his fellow servant fell down and pleaded with him, 'Have patience with me, and I will pay you.'"

Are there words you have caught yourself saying that you do not like when others say them? _____
_____
_____

30 "He refused and went and put him in prison until he should pay the debt. 31 When his fellow servants saw what had taken place, they were greatly distressed, and they went and reported to their master all that had taken place."

How could someone repay his or her debt while in prison?
_____
_____
_____

Was the servant wrong in wanting to be paid what was owed to him? _____
_____
_____

"And you know, when you've experienced grace and you feel like you've been forgiven, you're a lot more forgiving of other people. You're a lot more gracious to others."   Rick Warren

32 "Then his master summoned him and said to him, 'You wicked servant! I forgave you all that debt because you pleaded with me. 33 And should not you have had mercy on your fellow servant, as I had mercy on you?' 34 And in anger his master delivered him to the jailers, until he should pay all his debt."

Is wicked too harsh a term? _____

_____

_____

Define mercy and give an illustration. _____

_____

_____

_____

_____

35 "So also my heavenly Father will do to every one of you, if you do not forgive your brother from your heart."

What conditions are necessary for forgiveness? _____

_____

_____

_____

How can you forgive without encouraging irresponsibility?

_____

_____

_____

_____

The word forgiveness has the word "give" in the middle. Is this relevant? _____

_____

_____

Emmett Aldrich's has a conflict resolution ministry that focuses on peace. He strives to mediate between two parties to bring harmony. He lists Ten Keys to Forgiveness.

1. Let Go of the Anger
2. Don't be Stubborn
3. Stop Thinking of yourself as a Victim
4. Focus on the Future
5. Re-Learn to Trust
6. Be Reasonable in your expectations of Others
7. Expect that it will take time to Forgive
8. Examine your Heart
9. Let Forgiveness become an Everyday Practice
10. Ask God for Guidance

What points do you find helpful? _____
_____
_____

Are there any points that should be deleted or worded differently?
_____
_____
_____

"Forgiveness is about empowering yourself, rather than empowering your past." T. D. Jakes

FORGIVE GOD?: DEVOTION 1

PACO

Dr. Randy T. Johnson | Growth Pastor

I enjoy the movie, "Home Alone." There are great quotable lines like, "Keep the change you filthy animal." I also like the facial expression when Kevin puts on after-shave lotion. However, my favorite section is when Kevin meets the scary old man from across the street. They are in church and are starting to bond. The old man tells Kevin that he comes to church because it is the only way he can see his granddaughter. He does not even remember what he and his son fought about, but now they do not speak to each other. The old man wants his family back. Kevin tells him to try. I believe it is a beautiful picture of forgiving and being forgiven.

Matthew 18:21-22 gives the immediate context of The Unforgiving Servant, *"Then Peter came up and said to him, 'Lord, how often will my brother sin against me, and I forgive him? As many as seven times?' Jesus said to him, 'I do not say to you seven times, but seventy-seven times.'"* Rabbis taught that you only had to forgive someone three times. On the fourth time, you did not have to forgive the one who offended you. Peter was probably trying to impress Jesus. He says, "Seven times?" Jesus says, "Wow, I am impressed with you Peter. You are the man." No, Jesus shows His heart when He says, "seventy-seven times." We are not to keep track. We are to forgive because we have been forgiven so much more.

There is a story told about a boy in Spain named Paco who ran away from home. His father looked for him and counted the days waiting for him to return. Finally, he put an article in the Madrid newspaper saying something like, "Dear Paco, meet me in front of this newspaper office at noon on Saturday. All is forgiven. Love, Papa." On Saturday, 800 Pacos showed up.

I realize Paco is a common Spanish name, but I think the story goes much deeper. So many people want to be forgiven. Often both sides have some fault in the situation. It takes one person to speak up and say, "I am sorry. Please forgive me. You are forgiven."

Life is too short to live in hate and bitterness. It hurts us. God speaks as a loving Father when He tells us to forgive. It is to protect us and provide us from our self-destructive emotions. Forgiveness washes us.

Is there someone you need to ask to forgive you?

Is there someone you need to forgive?

FORGIVE GOD?: DEVOTION 2

THE GOAL

Dr. Randy T. Johnson | Growth Pastor

Merlin Olsen was a pro-football Hall of Fame defensive tackle. His job was to get to the quarterback, or whoever had the football, and tackle them. He was known as a very mild mannered man. After he retired, he even took a part on "Little House on the Prairie." Then there was Conrad Dobler. He was known as the dirtiest player in the NFL (Ironically, he played for the "Saints"). He was an offensive lineman. His job was to make sure no one got to his quarterback. He was known for hitting guys in the throat, holding them, kicking, and even biting players.

After Olsen's team had lost, he complained and criticized Dobler openly on air. When Dobler was questioned, he smiled and asked how many times Olsen got to his quarterback. The answer was none. Dobler said Olsen was so concerned about him that he forgot what his real goal was.

Yesterday, we looked at the immediate context of the parable of The Unforgiving Servant. However, there is a larger context. Matthew 18:15-17 gives what is known as the Matthew 18 Principle, *"If your brother sins against you, go and tell him his fault, between you and him alone. If he listens to you, you have gained your brother. But if he does not listen, take one or two others along with you, that every charge may be established by the evidence of two or three witnesses. If he refuses to listen to them, tell it to the church. And if he refuses to listen even to the church, let him be to you as a Gentile and a tax collector."*

The Matthew 18 Principle gives three steps to take when someone wrongs you. First, go to the person. If nothing happens, take a witness or two with you. Finally, if still no change, take it to the church. Sometimes people get so caught up in the process they forget the goal. The goal is to bring him back. It involves forgiveness. When someone wrongs us, the goal is to forgive and be reunited.

Maybe the Matthew 18 Principle should be known for forgiveness, not church discipline. The goal is not punishment. The goal is helping someone get right with Christ. Keep the goal in mind.

Does someone come to mind as you read this?

Have you talked to them about it?

Are you ready to forgive them?

FORGIVE GOD?: DEVOTION 3

KISSING FEET

Dr. Randy T. Johnson | Growth Pastor

Luke records thirty-five of Jesus' parables. Nineteen of these parables are only recorded in the Gospel according to Luke. The first one only recorded in Luke is about a creditor and two debtors. Luke 7:41-43 says, *"'A certain moneylender had two debtors. One owed five hundred denarii, and the other fifty. When they could not pay, he cancelled the debt of both. Now which of them will love him more?' Simon answered, 'The one, I suppose, for whom he cancelled the larger debt.' And he said to him, 'You have judged rightly.'"*

The parable seems pretty mild and basic. However, when you read the context of verse 36-40, we see Jesus is very precise and pointed in His speaking, *"One of the Pharisees asked him to eat with him, and he went into the Pharisee's house and reclined at the table. And behold, a woman of the city, who was a sinner, when she learned that he was reclining at table in the Pharisee's house, brought an alabaster flask of ointment, and standing behind him at his feet, weeping, she began to wet his feet with her tears and wiped them with the hair of her head and kissed his feet and anointed them with the ointment. Now when the Pharisee who had invited him saw this, he said to himself, 'If this man were a prophet, he would have known who and what sort of woman this is who is touching him, for she is a sinner.' And Jesus answering said to him, 'Simon, I have something to say to you.' And he answered, 'Say it, Teacher.'"*

The context totally explains the parable. Jesus is the forgiving creditor. Simon, representing all professionally righteous men, is the one who owed 50 denarii. The woman who was a sinner owed 500 denarii. Simon focused on being moral; she focused on worshipping the Lord.

Verses 44-46 get even more pointed, *"Then turning toward the woman he said to Simon, 'Do you see this woman? I entered your house; you gave me no water for my feet, but she has wet my feet with her tears and wiped them with her hair. You gave me no kiss, but from the time I came in she has not ceased to kiss my feet. You did not anoint my head with oil, but she has anointed my feet with ointment.'"* Simon should be embarrassed now. It appears he feels it was an honor for Jesus to be at his house, instead of realizing God Himself had entered the building.

Are you more concerned with being moral or worshipping God?

What are some ways you can worship God during the week?

FORGIVE GOD?: DEVOTION 4
TERRIFIC TESTIMONY
Dr. Randy T. Johnson | Growth Pastor

Several years ago I was asked to share my testimony at a conference. I was raised in a great Christian home, accepted Christ at age 7, baptized at age 12, rededicated my life in high school, and went to Bible College. During college, there was a time when I questioned whether to go after baseball or seminary. The rest is pretty basic.

The other speaker was Joe Ehrmann. Joe was an NFL all-star football player. He said he could always get a restaurant table wherever he wanted, whenever he wanted by reputation, force, or money. He was famous. He lived life big until his younger brother was diagnosed with Leukemia. Joe said he introduced himself to the doctor, so the doctor knew he was important. He bribed the doctor. Finally, he threatened the doctor. Nothing changed the diagnosis. His brother was going to die, and he could not do anything. He sat in the hospital hopeless. A random church group came by and asked if they could come in the room. They sang and shared the Gospel. He was 28, and it was the first time he ever heard the Gospel. He and his brother both gave their lives to Christ. Not long after, his brother died. It was a celebration, as they knew he would be in Heaven.

Luke 7:41-43 is a parable that describes the story of two people, *"'A certain moneylender had two debtors. One owed five hundred denarii, and the other fifty. When they could not pay, he cancelled the debt of both. Now which of them will love him more?' Simon answered, 'The one, I suppose, for whom he cancelled the larger debt.' And he said to him, 'You have judged rightly.'"*

Some would see Joe and me in this parable. However, it takes the same amount of God's forgiveness for everyone, and everyone should appreciate it the same. However, those who strayed longer often have a more radical transformation. It appears they *"love him more."* That should not be the case and it is not always the case, but the illustration makes sense. We all need to realize how lost we were without Jesus.

After the conference, Joe introduced himself to me. I mentioned how incredible his testimony was. He said mine was better. I was dumbfounded. He said, "Yours is the one I want for my children. I do not want them to have all the scars I have experienced." My testimony is remarkable.

What is your story? We all are born with a debt we cannot pay. Jesus picked up the bill. It is paid in full.

How will you thank Him today?

FORGIVE GOD?: DEVOTION 5

HACK INTO HOPE

Dr. Randy T. Johnson | Growth Pastor

I like acronyms. Payne Stewart was a Christian golfer who encouraged the bracelet that had G.O.L.F. on it. It meant God Offers Love and Forgiveness. He used it as a witnessing tool. His lifestyle and message were consistent, so this bracelet caught on in the golf world.

1 Timothy 1:1 gives a beautiful title for Jesus, *"Paul, an apostle of Christ Jesus by command of God our Savior and of Christ Jesus our hope."* Jesus is our Hope. He is Hope. He is our strength and confidence as we have Hope. We do not know what the future holds, but we know Who hold the future. He is Hope.

Philippians 4:13 focuses on Jesus, *"I can do all things through him who strengthens me."* I will not quit. I will press on confident that He brings hope. People need hope.

God has the future secure. We do not need to panic or fear. It is not always good for my blood pressure to watch a Michigan and Michigan State football game. However, if I DVR it and watch it after I know the results, it is fine. God loves us and holds the future. He is our Hope.

In Colossians 1:27 Jesus is called the Hope of Glory, *"To them God chose to make known how great among the Gentiles are the riches of the glory of this mystery, which is Christ in you, the hope of glory."* I know as a follower of Christ that I am going to Heaven when I die because He is the Hope of Glory.

I searched the web to find acronyms for Hope. One of the first ones I found everywhere was Hackers On Planet Earth. I thought it was funny. However, I found four other ones that touch the topic. Hope is to Have Only Positive Expectations. We can be positive because of who He is. Another one is Hold On, Pain Ends. I liked this one because we will go through difficulties, but we still can hold on. God gives us strength, purpose, and hope. John Maxwell uses an acronym of Hope that is very similar in encouraging people through Holding On, Praying Expectantly. Hope should affect our prayer life.

Finally, Hope means He Offers Peace Eternally. Jesus offers hope. He is Hope. If you do not know Him personally, today is the day to give your life to Him. If you already follow Him, remember the world needs Hope.

FORGIVE GOD?: DEVOTION 6

TEST INTO TESTIMONY

Dr. Randy T. Johnson | Growth Pastor

"And he cried to the Lord, and the Lord showed him a log, and he threw it into the water, and the water became sweet. There the Lord made for them a statute and a rule, and there he tested them, saying, 'If you will diligently listen to the voice of the Lord your God, and do that which is right in his eyes, and give ear to his commandments and keep all his statutes, I will put none of the diseases on you that I put on the Egyptians, for I am the Lord, your healer.'" Exodus 15:25-26

"The Lord, your healer" is Jehovah-Rapha. He is The Lord Who Heals. His specialty lies in the areas of spiritual, physical, and emotional. He makes us whole.

It must have been amazing to grab a log and throw it in the water. The water did not become okay; it became sweet. Bitter water became sweet. It would be great to bottle sweet water. Would it still have zero calories? It is important to notice the steps of faith Moses had to take. First, he had to be willing to throw a log in the water. I guess it was large enough that he needed to convince others to help him. Second, he has to drink potentially bitter water. He lived by faith and God acted.

In Psalm 103:3 God is the One *"who forgives all your iniquity, who heals all your diseases."* Psalm 147:3 continues the thought, *"He heals the brokenhearted and binds up their wounds."* He is the Lord, the Healer.

1 Peter 2:24 gives the ultimate healing, *"He himself bore our sins in his body on the tree, that we might die to sin and live*

to righteousness. By his wounds you have been healed." We are born with a seemingly incurable disease called sin. Nothing on earth can even slow it down. It is a death sentence, and if that is not bad enough, it carries over into the afterlife. God comes down from Heaven. He does not give a cure; He is the cure. However, He must die for us to live. He is the Lord, the Healer.

He turns our Pain into a Plan.

9

BOTTOM OF THE FIRST

Dr. Randy T. Johnson | Growth Pastor

When I was in college, I started off working in a shop from 5:00 pm to 4:30 am. I ground "snags" off the edges of pieces of metal, so the welders had smooth surfaces to work on. Later on, in college, Greyhound Bus Lines posted they were taking applications downtown. Over one thousand people applied and they hired twelve for training, and only two of us were offered positions. I took the position in information. I worked second shift as I answered phones (Sorry, I don't do a good Lily Tomlin impersonation). Soon after being hired in, I was promoted to supervisor.

I was appreciative to find a job when I went into the factory, but Greyhound doubled my wages, and the work was more in line with who I am.

What was your worst or toughest job? _____
_____
_____

What do you think is the toughest job? _____
_____
_____

Matthew 20:1-16 records the parable of the laborers in the vineyard.

1 For the kingdom of heaven is like a master of a house who went out early in the morning to hire laborers for his vineyard.

Who do you think is the master of the house? _____
_____
_____
_____

2 After agreeing with the laborers for a denarius a day, he sent them into his vineyard.

Who set the wages? _____
_____
_____

Are the laborers guaranteed to get hired that day? _____
_____
_____
_____

3 And going out about the third hour he saw others standing idle in the marketplace, 4 and to them he said, 'You go into the vineyard too, and whatever is right I will give you.'

Who set the wages? _____
_____
_____

5 So they went. Going out again about the sixth hour and the ninth hour, he did the same.

Are they desperate, foolish, or trusting of the master? _____
_____
_____
_____

6 And about the eleventh hour he went out and found others standing. And he said to them, 'Why do you stand here idle all day?' 7 They said to him, 'Because no one has hired us.' He said to them, 'You go into the vineyard too.'

How do you think these laborers felt? _____
_____
_____

Have you ever been in this situation? _____
_____
_____

8 And when evening came, the owner of the vineyard said to his foreman, 'Call the laborers and pay them their wages, beginning with the last, up to the first.'

Was it wrong to pay the last workers first? _____
_____
_____
_____

Was it a strategic business move to pay the last first? _____
_____
_____

***9** And when those hired about the eleventh hour came, each of them received a denarius.*

What would have been the tone or response of all involved (the Master, the foreman, the different work groups)? _____
_____
_____
_____

***10** Now when those hired first came, they thought they would receive more, but each of them also received a denarius. **11** And on receiving it they grumbled at the master of the house, **12** saying, 'These last worked only one hour, and you have made them equal to us who have borne the burden of the day and the scorching heat.' **13** But he replied to one of them, 'Friend, I am doing you no wrong. Did you not agree with me for a denarius? **14** Take what belongs to you and go. I choose to give to this last worker as I give to you. **15** Am I not allowed to do what I choose with what belongs to me? Or do you begrudge my generosity?'*

What would have been the tone or response of all involved (the Master, the foreman, the different work groups)? _____
_____
_____
_____

Is the master unjust, generous, or both? _____
_____
_____
_____

What should be the response of the first group? _____
_____
_____
_____

How does this parable relate to the Kingdom of God? _____
_____
_____
_____

16 So the last will be first, and the first last."

Does this verse have anything to do with Jews and Greeks?
_____
_____
_____

One of the most compelling stories I have heard that relates to this parable is the testimony of Ty Cobb. Ty Cobb was a hall-of-fame baseball player who played for the Detroit Tigers. He said, "Baseball was one-hundred percent of my life."

However, it is stated that he had a deathbed conversion when he said something like, "I wish I would have come to Christ in the top of the first instead of the bottom of the ninth."

What advantages are there of coming to Christ early in life?
_____
_____
_____

BOTTOM OF THE FIRST: DEVOTION 1

CAKE, ICING, AND GOD

Dr. Randy T. Johnson | Growth Pastor

I think John 3:16 is the cake, and John 10:10 is the icing. I will explain in a moment.

Matthew 20:1-16 contains the parable of a master who hires laborers to work in his vineyard. The first group is hired early in the morning and agreed on a denarius for a day's work. He also hired workers in the third hour, sixth hour, ninth hour, and even extremely late in the day at the eleventh hour. Everyone else was just happy to get work and did not negotiate a fee. Each person worked until the end of the day when it was time to get paid. He first paid those who started latest and gave them a denarius. He did this with the next three groups. When he came to the first group he hired, he gave them also a denarius. They were disappointed and expected more, but the agreement was for a denarius.

The same is true spiritually. Those who live a selfish, evil life, but accept Christ as Savior late in life receives the same benefit as those who accepted Christ at a young age and lived a faithful life. Both get Heaven.

The natural question is, "Why not have fun now and get saved later?"

I think John 3:16 is the cake, and John 10:10 is the icing. John 3:16 is the most famous verse in the Bible, and it reads, **"For God so loved the world, that he gave his only Son, that whoever believes in him should not perish but have eternal life."** The foundation of Christianity is solid on the promise of salvation through Jesus Christ. Our sin broke our relationship with God. He offers reconciliation through His Son's death. This reconciliation brings eternal life. John 10:10 gives the bonus of daily blessings, ***"The thief comes only to steal and kill and destroy. I came that they may have life and have it abundantly."*** Not only do we get eternal life and Heaven, but we are also offered life to the full. Jesus offers us abundant life.

Many of you probably answered that you should get saved today because no one is promised tomorrow (on earth). You are right, but also realize that salvation brings life to the full. We have value, purpose, and meaning in life.

Giving our life to Jesus brings salvation. Salvation brings God. God Himself (the Holy Spirit) dwells within us. This world does not have anything to offer that even comes close to that. It is a treat to put your trust in Jesus as young as one can.

"Oh, taste and see that the Lord is good! Blessed is the man who takes refuge in him!" (Psalm 34:8).

Cake? Icing? God?

BOTTOM OF THE FIRST: DEVOTION 2

COMFORT

Dr. Randy T. Johnson | Growth Pastor

People often say that becoming a Christian would be so much easier in the first century and that it would be easier to live consistently as a Christian in the first century. Seeing Jesus and being right with Him would cast all doubt. However, this is not accurate. Jesus limited His Deity so that He chose to only be in one place at a time. When He left, He sent the Holy Spirit to be with believers at all times. We receive comfort with Him indwelling us. Jesus' leaving was to our advantage.

John 16:7 says, **"Nevertheless, I tell you the truth: it is to your advantage that I go away, for if I do not go away, the Helper will not come to you. But if I go, I will send him to you."** It sounds out of place to hear Jesus saying that it is for our good that He went away. After He had left the earth, He sent the Holy Spirit back to His followers.

Matthew 20:1-16 records the parable of the master who hires workers for his vineyard at different times throughout the day, but ends up giving them the same pay. The earliest group to get hired felt he was unjust, but they miss that actually, he was showing grace. They also experienced his grace as they did not have a job and he hired them.

Let's revisit the question, "Why not have fun now and get saved later?"

After Jesus had left the earth, He sent the Holy Spirit back to His followers. Salvation brings comfort. John 14:16-17 reads, **"And I will ask the Father, and he will give you another Helper, to** *be with you forever, even the Spirit of truth, whom the world cannot receive, because it neither sees him nor knows him. You know him, for he dwells with you and will be in you."* Jesus gave us a Helper (Counselor, Comforter) to be with us all the time. We often go through times when we need comfort. So, Jesus gave us the Holy Spirit.

God comforts us in all our troubles. 2 Corinthians 1:3-4 says, *"Blessed be the God and Father of our Lord Jesus Christ, the Father of mercies and God of all comfort, 4 who comforts us in all our affliction, so that we may be able to comfort those who are in any affliction, with the comfort with which we ourselves are comforted by God."* God comforts His children. He is the loving Father.

I often hear people at funerals say, "I do not know how people without God get through this." Salvation brings hope, promises, and comfort.

BOTTOM OF THE FIRST: DEVOTION 3

SHREWD

Dr. Randy T. Johnson | Growth Pastor

Luke 16:1-9 gives the parable of the Unjust Steward. The story goes that a manager was caught wasting the owner's possessions. He does not want to be thrown out onto the streets to beg, so he has a plan. He goes to everyone who owes the owner money and agrees to a 50% discount if they pay right now. It works, and he is able to turn in a lot of money to the owner and save face. The owner was pleased. Verse 8 says, *"The master commended the dishonest manager for his shrewdness. For the sons of this world are more shrewd in dealing with their own generation than the sons of light."*

Jesus gives the explanation in verses 10-13, *"One who is faithful in a very little is also faithful in much, and one who is dishonest in a very little is also dishonest in much. If then you have not been faithful in the unrighteous wealth, who will entrust to you the true riches? And if you have not been faithful in that which is another's, who will give you that which is your own? No servant can serve two masters, for either he will hate the one and love the other, or he will be devoted to the one and despise the other. You cannot serve God and money."*

The manager was considered "shrewd." Google gives the definition, "Having or showing sharp powers of judgment; astute." It goes on to give an excellent list of synonyms: sharp-witted, sharp, smart, acute, intelligent, clever, canny, perceptive, perspicacious, sagacious, and wise.

The definition brings no negative connotation on being shrewd. In the back of my mind, I had a slight feeling of it being negative because Jesus said, *"Behold, I send you out as sheep in the midst of wolves; so be shrewd as serpents and innocent as doves"* (Matthew 10:16 NASB). Maybe I associate shrewd with serpents and serpents with Satan. But being shrewd is commendable. If we strive to be shrewd with money, how much more should we be with the souls of others? We read books, talk to friends, and even hire a professional in handling our money. How can we be shrewder in reaching others?

Who has God placed in your heart and mind?

What is your plan?

Be shrewd!

BOTTOM OF THE FIRST: DEVOTION 4

EXTRA MILE

Dr. Randy T. Johnson | Growth Pastor

Finding a good babysitter is hard. Typically we tried to use the grandparents. We are fortunate. We both knew you marry a family and not just a person. We are blessed. However, there were times when we needed some "outside" help. As a youth pastor and high school teacher, I knew potential babysitters. All situations went well, but we did have two babysitters who went through all of our cabinets (they did not cover it up well). We had another babysitter who got conned by our seven-year-old son to have a snack before bed that included cereal in chocolate milk. Finally, there was Amy.

Amy brought crafts for the kids, would read to them (she is now a teacher), got them to put their toys away, put them to bed, and cleaned the kitchen. We were just hoping for someone to "watch" the kids but got much more than we paid for. She went the extra mile.

Luke 17:7-10 gives a parable doing what is expected and doing more than just our duty, *"Will any one of you who has a servant plowing or keeping sheep say to him when he has come in from the field, 'Come at once and recline at table'? Will he not rather say to him, 'Prepare supper for me, and dress properly, and serve me while I eat and drink, and afterward you will eat and drink'? Does he thank the servant because he did what was commanded? So you also, when you have done all that you were commanded, say, 'We are unworthy servants; we have only done what was our duty.'"*

A servant was paid to work from sunrise to sunset. He was fortunate to have a way of earning some money. When he finished in the fields, he would come help in the house. It was his job. He got paid. There was not anything special.

In Matthew 5:41 in His Sermon on the Mount, Jesus talks about going the extra mile, ***"And if anyone forces you to go one mile, go with him two miles."*** Most people know the phrase and concept, but do not know where the extra mile concept came from or what it literally meant. In the first century, the Romans ruled Israel. Legally a Roman official could demand that a Jewish citizen carry his luggage a mile (some say they counted off 1,000 steps). It is even believed that Jews marked off a mile from their house so they knew where they could stop. Jesus was radical in saying to go the extra mile. Can you imagine the face of the Roman official as they started the second mile?

Is there something extra you can do for your family today?

Is there something extra you can do for a friend today?

Is there something extra (good) you should do for an enemy today?

Is there something extra you can do for the Lord today?

Go the extra mile!

BOTTOM OF THE FIRST: DEVOTION 5

RECHARGED

Dr. Randy T. Johnson | Growth Pastor

Recently one of my former students and golfers text me asking if I wanted to get together with him and golf. I immediately text him I would like it. We met that next Monday morning at the golf course. He "rolled up" on an electric bike with his golf clubs on a pull trailer. He had biked nine miles pulling clubs. He said it was easy because as he peddled the "battery" put out extra power propelling him to upwards of 20 miles per hour. He then just had to recharge it when he got home. I was very impressed.

Energy is a hot topic. There are all kinds of sources for energy beyond fuel. There is coal, oil, hydropower, nuclear power, solar energy, wind energy, and even nuclear power. I even heard that the E85 gas has corn as a base for its energy. There are even reports that chocolate can be used to produce energy. I know chocolate gives me some more energy.

Scripture calls Jesus the source of life in referring to Him as the True Vine.

John 15:1-7 says,
"I am the true vine, and my Father is the vinedresser. Every branch in me that does not bear fruit he takes away, and every branch that does bear fruit he prunes, that it may bear more fruit. Already you are clean because of the word that I have spoken to you. Abide in me, and I in you. As the branch cannot bear fruit by itself, unless it abides in the vine, neither can you, unless you abide in me. I am the vine; you are the branches. Whoever abides in me and I in him, he it is that bears much fruit, for apart from me you can do

nothing. If anyone does not abide in me he is thrown away like a branch and withers; and the branches are gathered, thrown into the fire, and burned. If you abide in me, and my words abide in you, ask whatever you wish, and it will be done for you."

We need to produce fruit. The only way we can produce fruit is by being connected to the True Vine, Jesus Christ. The word "abide" is used seven times in these seven verses. To abide means to remain. It emphasizes the idea of "being" not "doing." Being plugged into Jesus recharges us. John 8:31 says, **"So Jesus said to the Jews who had believed him, 'If you abide in my word, you are truly my disciples.'"**

Stay in the Word and let the Word dwell in you. It recharges us. It helps us get connected to the Ultimate Source in Jesus Christ.

BOTTOM OF THE FIRST: DEVOTION 6

BOSS

Dr. Randy T. Johnson | Growth Pastor

What thoughts cross your mind when you hear the word "boss?" I saw an acronym that said Built On Self Success. It is a pessimistic thought to think all bosses are selfish. We know Jesus was the ultimate leader and He led by serving. He washed the feet.

Adonai is the name of God that refers to Him as The Lord; My Great Lord. He is our Master, the majestic Lord, and our total authority. He is Boss.

Psalm 8 gives a beautiful portrait of Him.

"O Lord, our Lord,
  how majestic is your name in all the earth!
You have set your glory above the heavens.
2 Out of the mouth of babies and infants,
you have established strength because of your foes,
  to still the enemy and the avenger.
3 When I look at your heavens, the work of your fingers,
  the moon and the stars, which you have set in place,
4 what is man that you are mindful of him,
  and the son of man that you care for him?
5 Yet you have made him a little lower than the heavenly beings
  and crowned him with glory and honor.
6 You have given him dominion over the works of your hands;
  you have put all things under his feet,
7 all sheep and oxen,
  and also the beasts of the field,

8 the birds of the heavens, and the fish of the sea,
   whatever passes along the paths of the seas.
9 O Lord, our Lord,
   how majestic is your name in all the earth!"

God is amazing. Look at the sky tonight at sunset. The vibrant colors, the clouds, the moon with enough power to affect the oceans' tide, and the stars all lined up in design and formation.

Take a walk in a park or the woods. Examine nature. See the glory of God.

In Habakkuk 3:19 the title of Adonai is used again, **"God, the Lord, is my strength; he makes my feet like the deer's; he makes me tread on my high places."**

God is our strength. He cares about us. He loves us. I too wonder, "What is man that you are mindful of him?" However, He is mindful of us.

Praise Him! Worship Him! Look all around and see Him.

The awe we feel encourages our actions of obedience.

10

A-CHORE-ABLE

Dr. Randy T. Johnson | Growth Pastor

Our daughter is detailed oriented. My wife and I still enjoy talking about a pivotal day when our daughter was in seventh grade. She came home from school and asked who was in her room. My wife had been the only one home and asked, "Why?" She said, "You moved something." My wife just explained she had dusted her room. Our daughter then shocked us. She said, "If I dust my room, will you leave it alone?" That was a tough question. She then went on to agree to vacuum and do her laundry. Finally, she asked for the upstairs bathroom. She would clean it if her older brother had to use the downstairs bathroom. She kept her word and did a great job.

What chores did you have as a child? _____
_____
_____

At what age should children have certain chores? _____
_____
_____

Matthew 21:28-32 gives the Parable of Two Sons, but to fully understand it one needs to look at the preceding verses (23-27),

"And when he entered the temple, the chief priests and the elders of the people came up to him as he was teaching, and said, 'By what authority are you doing these things, and who gave you this authority?' 24 Jesus answered them, 'I also will ask you one question, and if you tell me the answer, then I also will tell you by what authority I do these things. 25 The baptism of John, from where did it come? From heaven or from man?' And they discussed it among themselves, saying, 'If we say, 'From heaven,' he will say to us, 'Why then did you not believe him?' 26 But if we say, 'From man,' we are afraid of the crowd, for they all hold that John was a prophet.' 27 So they answered Jesus, 'We do not know.' And he said to them, 'Neither will I tell you by what authority I do these things.'"

How many times is the word "authority" used in these five verses?
_____
_____
_____

What was the dilemma for the chief priests and elders over Jesus' question? _____
_____
_____

Do you have situations were you struggle between pleasing God and others? _____
_____
_____

Jesus then goes into a parable of Two Sons to make His point.

"What do you think? A man had two sons. And he went to the first and said, 'Son, go and work in the vineyard today.' 29 And he answered, 'I will not,' but afterward he changed his mind and went. 30 And he went to the other son and said the same. And he answered, 'I go, sir,' but did not go. 31 Which of the two did the will of his father?' They said, 'The first.' Jesus said to them, 'Truly, I say to you, the tax collectors and the prostitutes go into the kingdom of God before you. 32 For John came to you in the way of righteousness, and you did not believe him, but the tax collectors and the prostitutes believed him. And even when you saw it, you did not afterward change your minds and believe him.'"

What was the answer and response of the first son? _____
_____
_____
_____

How does this reflect the topic of authority? _____
_____
_____
_____

What was the answer and response of the second son? _____
_____
_____
_____

How does this reflect the topic of authority? _____
_____
_____
_____

How do the sons represent the Jewish leaders and the group of tax collectors and prostitutes? _____
_____
_____

"Rejection of parental authority is a rejection of God's authority. And the rejection of God's authority is, in fact, claiming his authority as my own. It is an attempt to be God." Pastor Paul David Tripp

"The very word authority has within it the word author. An author is someone who creates and possesses a particular work. Insofar as God is the foundation of all authority, He exercises that foundation because He is the author and the owner of His creation. He is the foundation upon which all other authority stands or falls." R.C. Sproul

A-CHORE-ABLE: DEVOTION 1

FIRST LOVE

Dr. Randy T. Johnson | Growth Pastor

Matthew 21:28-32

"What do you think? A man had two sons. And he went to the first and said, 'Son, go and work in the vineyard today.' And he answered, 'I will not,' but afterward he changed his mind and went. And he went to the other son and said the same. And he answered, 'I go, sir,' but did not go. Which of the two did the will of his father?' They said, 'The first.' Jesus said to them, 'Truly, I say to you, the tax collectors and the prostitutes go into the kingdom of God before you. For John came to you in the way of righteousness, and you did not believe him, but the tax collectors and the prostitutes believed him. And even when you saw it, you did not afterward change your minds and believe him.'"

The second son says he will work in the vineyard and then does not (maybe he wanted to get paid). This frustrates all of us. We want someone to be true to his or her word. The son starts off by recognizing his father's authority in replying obedience, but then ignores or snubs his father's authority by not backing up his words with some action.

The context of this passage centers on the authority of Jesus. This son represents the chief priests and elders (the Jews). They start off by saying they will keep every law, but then fall away and even question and refuse the authority of God (Jesus).

We can often see where our heart is by where our money goes.

Money can change us.

Colossians 4:14
"Luke the beloved physician greets you, as does Demas."

Philemon 1:24
"And so do Mark, Aristarchus, Demas, and Luke, my fellow workers."

Demas was a follower of Jesus working alongside Paul. He is even called a fellow worker. Then something happens.

2 Timothy 4:10
"For Demas, in love with this present world, has deserted me and gone to Thessalonica. Crescens has gone to Galatia, Titus to Dalmatia."

Demas started as a follower of the Lord but then fell in love with the world. He was like the son saying yes, but not willing to obey in action. He fell in love with the world and hence the things of the world. His talk became cheap. His actions were louder than his words.

Revelation 2:4
"But I have this against you, that you have abandoned the love you had at first."

Have you lost or forgotten your calling? Have you slipped away from the Lord? Does your life look like you have fallen out of love with the Lord?

Hebrews 12:1
"Therefore, since we are surrounded by so great a cloud of witnesses, let us also lay aside every weight, and sin which clings so closely, and let us run with endurance the race that is set before us."

Are you on the right path? Will you remain true to your testimony?

Does your walk match your talk?

A-CHORE-ABLE: DEVOTION 2

180 DEGREES

Dr. Randy T. Johnson | Growth Pastor

Matthew 21:28-32
"What do you think? A man had two sons. And he went to the first and said, 'Son, go and work in the vineyard today.' And he answered, 'I will not,' but afterward he changed his mind and went. And he went to the other son and said the same. And he answered, 'I go, sir,' but did not go. Which of the two did the will of his father?' They said, 'The first.' Jesus said to them, 'Truly, I say to you, the tax collectors and the prostitutes go into the kingdom of God before you. For John came to you in the way of righteousness, and you did not believe him, but the tax collectors and the prostitutes believed him. And even when you saw it, you did not afterward change your minds and believe him.'"

The first son says he will not work in the vineyard and then does. This becomes a relief for all of us. The son starts off by disrespecting his father's authority in replying negatively, but then honor's his father's authority by repenting seen in his action.

The context of this passage centers on the authority of Jesus. This son represents the tax collectors and prostitutes (the Gentiles). They start off by saying they will not keep every law. They live for him or herself. However, later they recognize the authority of God (Jesus), and their life is turned 180 degrees.

We can often see where our heart is by where our money goes.

Money can change us, and it can help us change others.

Luke 19:1-10

"He entered Jericho and was passing through. 2 And behold, there was a man named Zacchaeus. He was a chief tax collector and was rich. 3 And he was seeking to see who Jesus was, but on account of the crowd he could not, because he was small in stature. 4 So he ran on ahead and climbed up into a sycamore tree to see him, for he was about to pass that way. 5 And when Jesus came to the place, he looked up and said to him, 'Zacchaeus, hurry and come down, for I must stay at your house today.' 6 So he hurried and came down and received him joyfully. 7 And when they saw it, they all grumbled, 'He has gone in to be the guest of a man who is a sinner.' 8 And Zacchaeus stood and said to the Lord, 'Behold, Lord, the half of my goods I give to the poor. And if I have defrauded anyone of anything, I restore it fourfold.' 9 And Jesus said to him, 'Today salvation has come to this house, since he also is a son of Abraham. 10 For the Son of Man came to seek and to save the lost.'"

Zacchaeus was a thief and despised by the people (verse 7). He would have been known for overtaxing the people and pocketing money. Yet verse 8 shows something happened. He said he would give half of his money to the poor and quadruple the payment to anyone he wronged. What happened? He fell in love with the Lord. Angels were celebrating because **"Today salvation has come to this house."**

Money is the root of all kinds of evil, but it can be a tool. We can use it to encourage others. We do not have to be rich to make a difference in someone else's life.

Who can you help and how?

I was challenged by this quote from an IRS auditor, "The trick is to stop thinking of it as 'your' money."

Whose money is it?

A-CHORE-ABLE: DEVOTION 3

LOST?

Dr. Randy T. Johnson | Growth Pastor

Luke 15 gives the parables of the Lost Sheep, the Lost Coin, and the Lost Son. The story of the Lost Son is quite familiar. The younger son comes to his father and asks for his inheritance. I cannot imagine loathing my family to the point that all I want is their money and to leave. He was given his one-third (the older son always received two-thirds), and he left. He ate, drank and was merry to the point he almost wished he had died.

Did the son know he was lost? The Lost Sheep did not know it was lost and of course, the Lost Coin could not know. Did the son know he was lost?

Luke 15:15-16 says, *"So he went and hired himself out to one of the citizens of that country, who sent him into his fields to feed pigs. And he was longing to be fed with the pods that the pigs ate, and no one gave him anything."* I can only imagine what a Jewish audience is thinking when this son goes so low to be with pigs. Definitely, not kosher pigs. Pagan pigs. He must have fallen into the hands of Gentiles.

Finally, verse 17-19 convey the attitude that he finally realized how lost he was, *"But when he came to himself, he said, 'How many of my father's hired servants have more than enough bread, but I perish here with hunger! I will arise and go to my father, and I will say to him, 'Father, I have sinned against heaven and before you. I am no longer worthy to be called your son. Treat me as one of your hired servants.'"*

The son realized he sinned against his father, but also God Himself.

The story goes on to say that the son goes to his father who comes running to him. The father welcomes him back as a son. They have a special party honoring him. A robe, ring, shoes, and fatted calf are on order.

Verse 24 gives the father's response, ***"For this my son was dead, and is alive again; he was lost, and is found.' And they began to celebrate."*** I believe that is also the Father's response. People are dead. They are lost. They need to acknowledge their sin and helplessness. Then they are ready to receive salvation that is granted by the Father. We know this is through the work of Jesus Christ.

2 Timothy 2 talks about how we as believers need to act. We need to speak, show, and live the love of Christ. In verse 26 we are told why, ***"And they may come to their senses and escape from the snare of the devil, after being captured by him to do his will."***

The world is caught in the snare of the devil. We have family, friends, and neighbors who do not know they are lost. We need to help them as the Lost Son, ***"come to their senses and escape."***

We all have a similar testimony: "I once was lost but now am found.; was blind, but now I see."

Pray for someone today asking God that they would realize their need for salvation. They might not know they are lost.

A-CHORE-ABLE: DEVOTION 4

FINANCIALLY SUSTAIN-A-BOLOGNA

Dr. Randy T. Johnson | Growth Pastor

Yesterday I talked about the Lost Son. I know you ladies may have chimed in that men never admit they are lost. They call it "the scenic route," but will not stop and ask for directions. Remember, "It is a short cut." When all else fails, "It is the GPS's fault."

Today, I want to look at the other son. Almost half of the passage in Luke 15 addresses once the son returns home. The younger son comes home with a repentant heart. Verses 22-24 give the father's response, *"But the father said to his servants, 'Bring quickly the best robe, and put it on him, and put a ring on his hand, and shoes on his feet. And bring the fattened calf and kill it, and let us eat and celebrate. For this my son was dead, and is alive again; he was lost, and is found.' And they began to celebrate."* Salvation brought celebration.

Salvation should bring celebration; however, check the older brother's response in verse 28 when he hears the celebration, *"But he was angry and refused to go in. His father came out and entreated him."* He was angry. His brother is home. His brother is safe. I wonder why the anger. Is it based on financial reasons? Is he worried his brother will get part of "his" share of the inheritance? Obviously, it is spiritual. There is a realm of selfishness as he immediately pouts that dad never did "anything" for him. Poor little boy. Actually, he is a grown man and needs to take responsibility for his emotions and actions. Dad probably prayed every day for the Lost Son and big brother felt taken for granted. Fortunately, the father came to him, too. The father reiterates his reasoning in verse 32, *"It was fitting to celebrate and be glad, for this your brother was dead, and is alive; he*

was lost, and is found." I wonder if the older brother went to the party. Maybe he is a lost son and does not know it.

Do we celebrate when others get saved?

Do not answer too quickly. Let me explain why. I despise the phrase "financially sustainable." Recently I have talked to two pastors I respect from other churches. We were talking about ministry in a certain location, and both of them in separate meeting were not for the ministry because it was not "financially sustainable." They both used the phrase. Maybe I missed that conference. Do not get me wrong, I like a business strategy and Dave Ramsey principles, but is not there something about Christianity called "faith?"

Does the prison ministry excite you or do you think they deserve to be punished? Do you think they are faking being saved hoping to get a lesser sentence? Does your mind wonder on how the money, time, and resources could be better used? By the way, it is not financially sustainable.

Or, do you celebrate when someone gets saved?

Are you thinking, "Do not even get me started on the Recovery ministry?" Do you feel choices have consequences and they deserve what they are getting every day? Are they the one group that does not deserve God's grace?

Or, do you celebrate when someone gets saved?

Do you think the downtown outreach ministry is a waste of time? Does your mind quickly judge the adults that they just need to get a job and be responsible? By the way, it is not financially sustainable.

Or, do you celebrate when someone gets saved?

Are you worried that the bus ministry might bring unsaved kids to our church? These kids might say bad things, do bad things, break items, and even disrespect honorable adults. They are trouble. They are lost.

I too was lost, but now am found. I was blind, but now I see. I strive to celebrate when "the least of these" gets saved. None of us are more worthy than the other.

Celebrate!

A-CHORE-ABLE: DEVOTION 5
"LIE" DOWN IN THE ARMS OF TRUTH

Dr. Randy T. Johnson | Growth Pastor

Helmut Thielicke was a German Protestant theologian and professor. In his book, *A little exercise for young theologians*, said, "The chief reason for this is that in us men truth and love are seldom combined." He talks about the struggle men have with pride and how truth feeds this as we fall into the "joy of possession" of some certain thought others might not be able to attain. This does not mean truth should be avoided. We need truth.

I am relying on the seven-year statute of limitations as I confess that I did spank my children when they were young. As my Pastor friend says, "Children are like canoes, best steered with a paddle in the back." However, my children knew they would get a second swat if they lied. We all hate it when people lie to us.

Jesus is the Faithful and True Witness. We can take Him at His Word. Him being True allows me to "lie" down in faith that He will keep His Word. He brings comfort and confidence.

Jesus is faithful. Revelation 1:5 says, **"And from Jesus Christ the faithful witness, the firstborn of the dead, and the ruler of kings on earth. To him who loves us and has freed us from our sins by his blood."** The guilt of our sin was washed away by His blood. He then went a step further and is the Faithful Witness for us.

Revelation 3:14 uses the same phrase for Jesus, **"And to the angel of the church in Laodicea write: 'The words of the Amen, the faithful and true witness, the beginning of God's creation.'"** He is the Faithful and True Witness.

Remember who comes in on the white horse? Revelation 19:11 tells us, *"Then I saw heaven opened, and behold, a white horse! The one sitting on it is called Faithful and True, and in righteousness he judges and makes war."* I do not know if there is a better description for a judge. He is faithful and true. I would vote for him.

Finally, John 14:6 says it all, *"Jesus said to him, 'I am the way, and the truth, and the life. No one comes to the Father except through me.'"* It is interesting that most people emphasize Jesus being the way and the life. We point out there is no other way to the Father (Heaven). We highlight life. Jesus is life and gives life, life to the full and eternal life. However, a key foundation to all of this is that it is true and He is the Truth.

Jesus being the Faithful and True Witness allows us to "lie" down in faith that He will keep His Word. He brings comfort and confidence as we receive His promises.

A-CHORE-ABLE: DEVOTION 6

I AM

Dr. Randy T. Johnson | Growth Pastor

Can you hear Popeye singing?
"I yam what I yam and I yam what I yam that I yam
And I got a lotta muscle and I only gots one eye
And I'll never hurt nobodys and I'll never tell a lie
Top to me bottom and me bottom to me top
That's the way it is 'til the day that I drop, what am I?
I yam what I yam."

He can bring a chuckle as he slaughters the English language and any clear pronunciation. However, he uses the phrase "I am." I will go along with it, as we should also be real and transparent. What you see is what I am and what you get. However, in Scripture the phrase and title "I Am" brings much, much more to the table.

Jehovah is the great "I Am." He is "The One Who Is." He has no starting or ending point. He is. He never changes. His promises never fail. When we are faithless, He is faithful.

The title is used in Exodus 3:14 when, *"God said to Moses, 'I am who I am.' And he said, 'Say this to the people of Israel, 'I am has sent me to you.'"* There should be a holy pause after we hear *"I am who I am."*

Psalm 102 is described as, *"A Prayer of one afflicted, when he is faint and pours out his complaint before the Lord."* We have all experienced affliction, tough times. These are the times we cry out to God. Verses 1-11 express the emotions and pain that the writer is experiencing. However, he has confidence because of who the Lord is. Verse 12 says, *"But you, O Lord, are enthroned forever; you are remembered throughout all generations."*

The first three words of verse 13 are so comforting, ***"You will arise."*** We can know that God will be there for us. He will arise.

Verses 17-21 speak of His actions are our response in praise, ***"He regards the prayer of the destitute and does not despise their prayer. Let this be recorded for a generation to come, so that a people yet to be created may praise the Lord: that he looked down from his holy height; from heaven the Lord looked at the earth, to hear the groans of the prisoners, to set free those who were doomed to die, that they may declare in Zion the name of the Lord, and in Jerusalem his praise."***

Finally, the chapter ends with a description of the "I Am" and how He will care for His people, ***"But you are the same, and your years have no end. The children of your servants shall dwell secure; their offspring shall be established before you"*** (verses 27-28).

At one point Popeye humorously says, "If I was gonna be Swee' Pea's mother, I should've at least let Olive be his father. Or viska versa. I ain't man enough to be no mother." He is not man enough to be a mother. Sounds pretty simple. However, he actually is not "man enough" to say, "I Yam What I Yam & Dats What I Yam!" Only the living God is the I Am.

11

TWO SLOTHS

Dr. Randy T. Johnson | Growth Pastor

What do you buy for someone who has everything? Maybe the question should be, what do you buy for someone who can afford whatever they want? If they want it, they already have it. These are the questions asked by people who meet the President, the Pope, or the Queen of England. It is customary to give a gift when you meet a dignitary.

The Huffington Post out of the United Kingdom lists some of the craziest gifts Queen Elizabeth has received over the years. A few of the items are a bag of salt, two sloths, a wine cooler that looks like a grasshopper, a framed origami bird, a box of mud (silver box with dirt from the WWI battlefields), cowboy boots, and horse semen (from a prized stud). Some of these might seem out of place, but they are probably better than Bolivian President Evo Morales' gift to Pope Francis. He gave the pope a crucifix fashioned as a communist-style hammer and sickle.

What is the craziest gift you have ever heard of? _____
_____
_____
_____

What idea of a gift would you have for someone like the President?
_____
_____
_____

I believe the best thing you can do for someone is to do something nice for his or her spouse or children. I also believe the worst thing you can do to someone is to hurt his or her spouse or children.

Matthew 21:33-45 records the parable of the wicked servants. See how they treated the master's son.

Hear another parable. There was a master of a house who planted a vineyard and put a fence around it and dug a winepress in it and built a tower and leased it to tenants, and went into another country.

Who do you think the master represents? _____
_____
_____
_____

What does the vineyard, fence, and tower represent individually?
_____
_____
_____

34 When the season for fruit drew near, he sent his servants to the tenants to get his fruit. 35 And the tenants took his servants and beat one, killed another, and stoned another. 36 Again he sent other servants, more than the first. And they did the same to them.

Who do the servants represent? _____
_____
_____

Do you have any unique situations when you let someone housesit or babysit? _____
_____
_____

Hebrews 11:36-38 is part of the Hall of Fame of Faith. Look what some servants of God went through, *"Others suffered mocking and flogging, and even chains and imprisonment. They were stoned, they were sawn in two, they were killed with the sword. They went about in skins of sheep and goats, destitute, afflicted, mistreated— of whom the world was not worthy—wandering about in deserts and mountains, and in dens and caves of the earth."*

What does the phrase *"of whom the world was not worthy"* mean? _____
_____
_____

What kind of persecution could we suffer in America today?
_____
_____
_____

"Suffering saints are living seed." Charles Spurgeon

37 Finally he sent his son to them, saying, 'They will respect my son.' 38 But when the tenants saw the son, they said to themselves, 'This is the heir. Come, let us kill him and have his inheritance.' 39 And they took him and threw him out of the vineyard and killed him.

Who does the son represent? _____
_____
_____

Does the son's inheritance refer to anything specific? _____
_____
_____
_____

At what point does the crowd catch on to the meaning? _____
_____
_____
_____

40 When therefore the owner of the vineyard comes, what will he do to those tenants?" 41 They said to him, "He will put those wretches to a miserable death and let out the vineyard to other tenants who will give him the fruits in their seasons."

Do the "other tenants" represent anyone? _____
_____
_____
_____

*42 Jesus said to them, "Have you never read in the Scriptures:
'The stone that the builders rejected
   has become the cornerstone;
this was the Lord's doing,
   and it is marvelous in our eyes'?*

What is a cornerstone? _____
_____
_____

How should Jesus being the Chief Cornerstone affect our lives?
_____
_____
_____

"Few people seem to realize that the resurrection of Jesus is the cornerstone to a worldview that provides the perspective to all of life."   Josh McDowell

43 Therefore I tell you, the kingdom of God will be taken away from you and given to a people producing its fruits. 44 And the one who falls on this stone will be broken to pieces; and when it falls on anyone, it will crush him."

What do the "fruits" represent? _____
_____
_____

45 When the chief priests and the Pharisees heard his parables, they perceived that he was speaking about them.

Why did they not repent and follow Him? _____
_____
_____
_____

Why did they not arrest Him? _____
_____
_____

What do you get God who has everything?

Do not focus on dying for Him; live for Him.

TWO SLOTHS: DEVOTION 1

LOVE ME, LOVE MY SON

Dr. Randy T. Johnson | Growth Pastor

I remember back in the day when the California Angels had two pitchers who could throw over 100 mph. The first one became a Texan legend, Nolan Ryan. The second one people forgot about because he threw his arm out and had to have surgery. This guy could not ever throw the same again, but played some 20 seasons. He was even with the Tigers from 1988-1992. It was funny to watch the speed gun after his injury when he made it back to the mound. He threw junk pitches with a big curve. Often the radar would read the catcher's throw back to Tanana higher than the pitch itself. He is Frank Tanana, or as Ernie Harwell use to say "Tan-talzing Tanana."

The neatest thing about Frank Tanana is his faith. He accepted Christ as a pro player and it changed his life. In the late 80's when he was in Detroit, I contacted him and asked if he could share some thoughts with my youth group before or after a game. He agreed. It was awesome. The kids took in every word as he and his wife, Cathy, shared sound biblical truths. I will forever be grateful. My dilemma was, "What could I get him of value that he would not already have?" Obviously, the youth made fun thank you cards, but instead of getting him "another" baseball, we decided to get a nice bouquet of flowers for his wife.

One of the best ways to encourage someone is to do something nice for his or her spouse or children. Matthew 21:33-41 shows the opposite can be true, too. *"Hear another parable. There was a master of a house who planted a vineyard and put a fence around it and dug a winepress in it and built a tower and leased it to tenants, and went into another country. When the season for fruit drew near, he sent his servants to the tenants to get his fruit. And the tenants took his servants and beat one, killed another, and stoned another. Again he sent other servants, more than the first. And they did the same to them. Finally he sent his son to them, saying, 'They will respect my son.' But when the tenants saw the son, they said to themselves, 'This is the heir. Come, let us kill him and have his inheritance.' And they took him and threw him out of the vineyard and killed him. When therefore the owner of the vineyard comes, what will he do to those tenants? They said to him, 'He will put those wretches to a miserable death and let out the vineyard to other tenants who will give him the fruits in their seasons.'"*

I am sure the "owner of the vineyard" was surprised, hurt, and mad when the tenants beat and killed his servants. However, once they touched his son, it was game on. He did not just fire them, he *"put those wretches to a miserable death."*

I learned an interesting principle early in life: Do not break up a fight between brothers. They will switch their emotions and turn on you. Blood is thicker than water.

To do something nice for someone, do it for their his or her family. I am reminded of Matthew 25:40, *"And the King will answer them, 'Truly, I say to you, as you did it to one of the least of these my brothers, you did it to me.'"* I think the logic goes, doing something nice for someone else is like doing it for Jesus which is like doing it for God Himself.

TWO SLOTHS: DEVOTION 2

ROCK YOUR WORLD

Dr. Randy T. Johnson | Growth Pastor

Rob, a friend of mine, recently told me about a "Joshua Tray." I was confused. He went on to describe how parents are putting stones on a tray (you or your kids can decorate the tray however you want). The stones have "words" on them. "Whenever God answers a prayer or does something special for you, you add a stone with a word on it to remind you." Ever so often, you pull out the tray and have each child pick a rock. You then tell the story. Rob said that as parents we are missing a crucial time to let our children know what God has done for us.

Another friend puts rocks or plants a tree as a reminder of pivotal points of life. He can walk his yard or just look out the back window and praise God.

Children will not remember or see how God has blessed if we do not help.

The concept comes from Joshua 4:4-6 when the Israelites are going to cross the Jordan River, *"Then Joshua called the twelve men from the people of Israel, whom he had appointed, a man from each tribe. And Joshua said to them, 'Pass on before the ark of the LORD your God into the midst of the Jordan, and take up each of you a stone upon his shoulder, according to the number of the tribes of the people of Israel, that this may be a sign among you. When your children ask in time to come, 'What do those stones mean to you?'"*

The stones were intended as a sign for them. It was to be a continual reminder of how awesome our God is.

The parable of the wicked tenants in Matthew 21:33-45 refers to stones three times. The vineyard had a fence around it, which would have been made of stones. There was a tower built of stones. Finally, verses 42-45 say, **"Jesus said to them, 'Have you never read in the Scriptures: 'The stone that the builders rejected has become the cornerstone; this was the Lord's doing, and it is marvelous in our eyes'? Therefore I tell you, the kingdom of God will be taken away from you and given to a people producing its fruits. And the one who falls on this stone will be broken to pieces; and when it falls on anyone, it will crush him.' When the chief priests and the Pharisees heard his parables, they perceived that he was speaking about them."**

The most crucial stone is the cornerstone. Jesus is the Chief Cornerstone. It is the foundation everything is built off. It is the pivotal piece. Nowadays the "cornerstone" is more of a marquee with a dedication or date on it. It is a reminder stone of someone or a time period.

The cornerstone of our life needs to be Jesus Christ. Every other "stone" needs to build off of Him. Every purchase, relationship, and decision is laid based on what fits best in His plan. This is not just a stone to remind us of the past, but He is to direct our future.

What decision are you struggling with right now? Think and pray what God would want. Work every decision through Him and then create reminder stones of the blessings that come.

TWO SLOTHS: DEVOTION 3

PRAY UP

Dr. Randy T. Johnson | Growth Pastor

Luke 18:9-14 records a parable on prayer: *"He also told this parable to some who trusted in themselves that they were righteous, and treated others with contempt: 'Two men went up into the temple to pray, one a Pharisee and the other a tax collector. The Pharisee, standing by himself, prayed thus: 'God, I thank you that I am not like other men, extortioners, unjust, adulterers, or even like this tax collector. I fast twice a week; I give tithes of all that I get.' But the tax collector, standing far off, would not even lift up his eyes to heaven, but beat his breast, saying, 'God, be merciful to me, a sinner!' I tell you, this man went down to his house justified, rather than the other. For everyone who exalts himself will be humbled, but the one who humbles himself will be exalted.'"*

Prayer is a matter of heart. Too often we come to prayer judging others and clearly prideful. Other times we pray through our schedule asking God just to follow us and bless. Then there are the times we pray and do not even remember we prayed because our mind was all over the place. Finally, there are those sweet times we have a conversation with God Himself.

I have a simple prayer I like to pray. I use it to exalt God. I use it to get refocused on what is important. I pray it when I am overwhelmed.

"Lord Jesus Christ, Son of God
Have mercy on me a sinner."

I do not know the history of the prayer or if it has a special name. I do not think it is a "special secretive prayer" that puts people in a certain presence of God. I use it to remind myself that He is God and I am not. The world revolves around the "Son", not me.

I use a breathing strategy that emphasizes my heart. I inhale while saying the first phrase. It lifts my head and heart in praising, "Lord Jesus Christ, Son of God." Then I exhale lowering my head in humility and submission saying, "Have mercy on me a sinner."

I have been criticized for this prayer because "Jesus does not see me as a sinner anymore." They quote or email Hebrews 4:16 saying, "Let us then with confidence draw near to the throne of grace, that we may receive mercy and find grace to help in time of need." I approach with confidence, but with respect. Maybe you would be more comfortable with:

"Lord Jesus Christ, Son of God
Lead me your faithful servant."

My goal is not to belittle children of God, but to exalt my Savior.

I encourage praying this prayer with full breaths while worshipping Him. I have found that even a couple minutes calm my mind and spirit. It calms me, purifies me, and refocuses me.

TWO SLOTHS: DEVOTION 4

GOD-MADE MAN

Dr. Randy T. Johnson | Growth Pastor

"Two men went up into the temple to pray, one a Pharisee and the other a tax collector. The Pharisee, standing by himself, prayed thus: 'God, I thank you that I am not like other men, extortioners, unjust, adulterers, or even like this tax collector. I fast twice a week; I give tithes of all that I get.' But the tax collector, standing far off, would not even lift up his eyes to heaven, but beat his breast, saying, 'God, be merciful to me, a sinner!' I tell you, this man went down to his house justified, rather than the other. For everyone who exalts himself will be humbled, but the one who humbles himself will be exalted" (Luke 18:10-14).

I should be thrilled with the simple prayer of salvation that the tax collector makes; however, I do not let that sink in long enough. I get so caught up with how much the Pharisee's prayer bothers me. I think about it so much that I miss the context. Verse 9 bothers me even more, **"He also told this parable to some who trusted in themselves that they were righteous, and treated others with contempt."**

Did you catch the phrase? They **"trusted in themselves that they were righteous."** At least three things bother me about that phrase.

First, it makes man the judge. James 4:12 says, **"There is only one lawgiver and judge, he who is able to save and to destroy. But who are you to judge your neighbor?"** God is the only Judge who can save and destroy. Man is only a wanna-be so that he can feel good comparing himself to those who do not appear to measure up. His verdict is that he is righteous.

Second, this phrase reeks of pride. Proverbs 11:2 says, **"When pride comes, then comes disgrace, but with the humble is wisdom."** Pride goes before a fall. By trusting in themselves, they will fall.

Finally, this phrase reminds me of guys who say they are a "self-made man." By being self-made, they sell themselves short. It is better to be God-made. Psalm 139:13-14 say, **"For you formed my inward parts; you knitted me together in my mother's womb. I praise you, for I am fearfully and wonderfully made. Wonderful are your works; my soul knows it very well."** God made us, that is what makes us special.

The irony goes something like this, if you did come from a "meaningless" start into someone "important," is it not because God created you with the spunk necessary. Therefore, did God make you "self-made?"

I have realized that if you see any fault in me, I am to blame. If there is anything noteworthy, it is from God alone. I am a God-made man.

Revelation 4:11 gives an appropriate conclusion, **"Worthy are you, our Lord and God, to receive glory and honor and power, for you created all things, and by your will they existed and were created."**

TWO SLOTHS: DEVOTION 5

YOU ARE YOUR FATHER'S SON

Dr. Randy T. Johnson | Growth Pastor

I remember as a child going to K-Mart hoping for a great "Blue-Light Special." Ever so often the store would announce an unadvertised sale in a particular section of the store "for the next five minutes." It was fun.

We did not have cell phones, so as we entered the store my mom would usually say, "I will meet you up front in fifteen minutes." If she forgot, she could embarrass us by paging us or just look for us. I was regularly trying on every baseball glove, even the left-handed ones, smacking my fist into the palm. Mom knew where to look.

In Luke 2 Joseph and Mary realize Jesus is no longer with them. They look for three days. Stop and think through that. Emotions probably go from anger, to fear, to even panic. When they find Him, they ask why He left them. In verse 49 we read, ***"And he said to them, 'Why were you looking for me? Did you not know that I must be in my Father's house?'"***

If you were in K-Mart, you would wonder where to look for your child. Are they in the toy section, trying on shoes, checking out the books, or playing one of the quarter games in the front of the store? Your mind would race. A city would be much harder.

The other place to find me would have been as my dad's shadow. I would follow him everywhere.

Jesus asks, "Where did you expect to find Me?" He wanted to be with His Father. He is the Son of God!

Luke 1:35 says, ***"And the angel answered her, 'The Holy Spirit will come upon you, and the power of the Most High will overshadow you; therefore the child to be born will be called holy—the Son of God.'"*** He did not become the Son of God. He was always Him.

Luke continues in 1:32 saying, ***"He will be great and will be called the Son of the Most High. And the Lord God will give to him the throne of his father David."***

Hebrews 4:14 adds, ***"Since then we have a great high priest who has passed through the heavens, Jesus, the Son of God, let us hold fast our confession."*** The author just naturally refers to Jesus as the Son of God.

Jesus is the Son of God. He wanted to spend time with His Father. When you spend time with your dad you start sounding like him, you think like him, and you act like him.

John 1:12 is amazing, ***"But to all who did receive him, who believed in his name, he gave the right to become children of God."*** Jesus is God, and He allows us to be adopted into the family. We should spend time with Dad. We will start talking like Him, thinking like Him, and act or respond the way He would.

I loved hearing people say, "You are your father's son."

TWO SLOTHS: DEVOTION 6

THE LORD OF HOSTS

Dr. Randy T. Johnson | Growth Pastor

In 1 Samuel 1:3 Samuel's dad is referenced, *"Now this man used to go up year by year from his city to worship and to sacrifice to the LORD of hosts at Shiloh, where the two sons of Eli, Hophni and Phinehas, were priests of the LORD."* He went to worship the Lord of Hosts. He went to worship Jehovah-Sabaoth, the Lord of Hosts, the Lord of Armies.

I wondered why God would emphasize His army? I know that one with God is a majority. He is God! He does not need an army, yet He is called the Lord of Hosts several times.

In David's fight with Goliath, 1 Samuel 17:45 says, *"Then David said to the Philistine, 'You come to me with a sword and with a spear and with a javelin, but I come to you in the name of the LORD of hosts, the God of the armies of Israel, whom you have defied.'"* David is going into battle and knows he is fighting for and with the Lord of Hosts.

I believe the name Lord of Hosts is important because it emphasizes God's character of justice. He does not just sit back in "love" and let anyone do anything to His people. He will go to battle with them and even for them.

Psalm 46:7 says, *"The LORD of hosts is with us; the God of Jacob is our fortress. Selah."* Life is not easy. God is watching over us. In Malachi 1:10-14 God is referred to as the Lord of Hosts four times. The passage closes with the statement, *"For I am a great King, says the LORD of hosts, and my name will be feared among the nations."* He is the Great King (even King of kings) and the Lord of Hosts.

I was surprised to find that the title Lord of Hosts is used some 232 times in Scripture. It is even used in the New Testament. James 5:4 says, **"Behold, the wages of the laborers who mowed your fields, which you kept back by fraud, are crying out against you, and the cries of the harvesters have reached the ears of the Lord of hosts."** I remember as a kid using the phrase, "Those sound like fightin' words." When God's people are hurt, their cry out to Him draws up the Lord of Hosts because "Those are fightin' words."

Lord of Hosts brings a particular classification with it. I have people who call me "Coach." They know me from a different arena than those who call me "Prof" or "Professor." God wears many hats. They are emphasized through His titles. Here He is basically "The General."

One with God is a majority. Romans 8:31 is so comforting and compelling, **"What then shall we say to these things? If God is for us, who can be against us?"**

God is with and for His children.

I admire and am challenged by Abraham Lincoln's words when asked if God was on his side, "Sir, my concern is not whether God is on our side; my greatest concern is to be on God's side, for God is always right."

God will be there for us. Can He count on us?

12

THE INVITATION

Dr. Randy T. Johnson | Growth Pastor

A lot of planning typically goes into a wedding. First, you want to make sure you pick the right person. Okay, that was obvious. Next, when to get married typically takes a lot of things into consideration. The most common wedding day of all time was July 7, 2007. Yes, 7-7-7. Third, you want to figure out your budget. The average cost for a wedding is just under $30,000. It is about the same price as a ladder and a new pickup truck for the elopement. Fourth, and maybe much earlier, you look at rings. According to the National Jeweler, the average couple spends about $6,000 on rings (hers is probably 90% of that amount). I remember hearing that we wear the ring on a specific finger because it was believed that the vein there went directly to the heart. When Angela and I were getting married 33 years ago, the nurse could not find a vein in my arm, so they had to take it from the vein in the back of my hand. Somewhere in the list is a theme, location, colors, cake, flowers, and eventually the guest list.

What are some of the craziest things you have seen or heard about a wedding? _____

_____

_____

What are some of the most meaningful aspecets you have seen or heard about a wedding? _____
_____
_____

The guest list can be difficult. There are the people you need to invite, but know will not be able to make it. Then you need to add in the plus ones. Finally, your parents get involved, and you end up finding out that 50% of the people at your wedding you do not even know.

Matthew 22:1-14 contains the parable of a wedding feast and the changing guest list, **"And again Jesus spoke to them in parables, saying, 'The kingdom of heaven may be compared to a king who gave a wedding feast for his son.'"**

What is the Kingdom of Heaven? _____
_____
_____

"There is no more lovely, friendly or charming relationship, communion or company, than a good marriage." Martin Luther

3 "and sent his servants to call those who were invited to the wedding feast, but they would not come."

What are some valid reasons for not going to a wedding? _____
_____
_____
_____

Would you ever miss a wedding because you did not approve of the wedding? _____
_____
_____

4 "Again he sent other servants, saying, 'Tell those who are invited, 'See, I have prepared my dinner, my oxen and my fat calves have been slaughtered, and everything is ready. Come to the wedding feast.'"

Do you appreciate that the King often sends the invitation more than once? _____
_____
_____

What are some reasons why it may be important to have guests at the wedding? _____
_____
_____

"A married person does not live in isolation. He or she has made a promise, a pledge, a vow, to another person. Until that vow is fulfilled and the promise is kept, the individual is in debt to his marriage partner. That is what he owes. "You owe it to yourself" is not a valid excuse for breaking a marriage vow but a creed of selfishness." R.C. Sproul

5 "But they paid no attention and went off, one to his farm, another to his business, 6 while the rest seized his servants, treated them shamefully, and killed them."

Who is Jesus talking about? Who was invited and who was killed?
_____
_____
_____

7 "The king was angry, and he sent his troops and destroyed those murderers and burned their city. 8 Then he said to his servants, 'The wedding feast is ready, but those invited were not worthy.'"

What does the phrase *"not worthy"* mean here? _____
_____
_____
_____

9 "'Go therefore to the main roads and invite to the wedding feast as many as you find.' 10 And those servants went out into the roads and gathered all whom they found, both bad and good. So the wedding hall was filled with guests."

Who would the *"bad and good"* refer to? _____
_____
_____

11 "But when the king came in to look at the guests, he saw there a man who had no wedding garment. 12 And he said to him, 'Friend, how did you get in here without a wedding garment?' And he was speechless."

What do the wedding garments represent? _____
_____
_____
_____

How would this apply today? _____
_____
_____

13 "Then the king said to the attendants, 'Bind him hand and foot and cast him into the outer darkness. In that place there will be weeping and gnashing of teeth.'"

What location is described here? _____
_____
_____

What does this imply about the wedding garment and that guest?
_____
_____
_____

14 "For many are called, but few are chosen."

How does this phrase relate to the parable? _____
_____
_____
_____

"Many people spend more time in planning the wedding than they do in planning the marriage." Zig Ziglar

THE INVITATION: DEVOTION 1

WEDDING VOWS

Dr. Randy T. Johnson | Growth Pastor

Matthew 22:2-10 gives the parable of a wedding feast, *"The kingdom of heaven may be compared to a king who gave a wedding feast for his son, and sent his servants to call those who were invited to the wedding feast, but they would not come. Again he sent other servants, saying, 'Tell those who are invited, 'See, I have prepared my dinner, my oxen and my fat calves have been slaughtered, and everything is ready. Come to the wedding feast.' But they paid no attention and went off, one to his farm, another to his business, while the rest seized his servants, treated them shamefully, and killed them. The king was angry, and he sent his troops and destroyed those murderers and burned their city. Then he said to his servants, 'The wedding feast is ready, but those invited were not worthy. Go therefore to the main roads and invite to the wedding feast as many as you find.' And those servants went out into the roads and gathered all whom they found, both bad and good. So the wedding hall was filled with guests."*

Christ will come back for His bride, the church. We need to be ready. Several parables and verses address that magnificent wedding. I find it interesting to see the struggle that can be involved in wedding vows. Some just want to say, "I will" or "I do." Others want to write their own. Both members do not often agree.

Frank Powell writes an article on "12 Truthful Marriage Vows You Won't Hear At A Wedding."

1. I promise to never flirt, lust, or desire the attention of someone of the opposite sex.
2. I promise to never expect a 50/50 marriage.
3. I promise to make the Gospel the mission of our marriage.
4. I promise to love who you are today, not what I want you to be.
5. I promise you will never be responsible for my happiness.
6. I promise to make my expectations clear.
7. I promise to never say "I forgive you" unless I truly mean it.
8. I promise to be for you, to encourage your dreams, to help you become the man or woman God created you to be.
9. I promise to never complain about our marriage, in general, or you, in particular, to others.
10. I promise to believe the best is yet to come, regardless of how good or bad things are today.
11. I promise to protect our marriage from outside influences, including kids, work, and in-laws.
12. I promise to surround our marriage with a community of Christians who will encourage and support us.

I think this list should be a good reminder to all of us as we regularly renew our vows. Wedding vows are important. They are a covenant and promise before witnesses between a man and woman. They also involve God.

Have you ever thought about saying your wedding vows to Christ Himself?

I _____, take you, Jesus, to be my wedded Husband. To have and to hold, from this day forward, for better, for worse, for richer, for poorer, in sickness or in health, to love and to cherish till death do us part. And hereto I pledge you my faithfulness.
You can skip the "till death do us part." He offers eternal life!

THE INVITATION: DEVOTION 2

BLACK TIE OPTIONAL

Dr. Randy T. Johnson | Growth Pastor

I often struggle what to wear to a wedding. Couples are striving to be more and more creative. With vows taking place underwater or high above while skydiving or bunging jumping, everyone would be confused. However, I am not sure with the "cowboy" theme if I wear jeans with a sports jacket. Also, are there special rules for outside weddings? I still think tennis shoes with a tuxedo do not make sense. By the way, "black tie optional" probably will not happen with me. It might be easier for women, just do not wear white. My biggest challenge in what to wear at a wedding is not to look too much better than the groom.

Matthew 22:2-14 contains the parable of the wedding feast. A king sends out several invites, but the anticipated crowd does not show up. Therefore, who goes to an unexpected group and invites them. Everything seems to go well until the king notices something. Verses 11-14 describe the scene, *"But when the king came in to look at the guests, he saw there a man who had no wedding garment. And he said to him, 'Friend, how did you get in here without a wedding garment?' And he was speechless. Then the king said to the attendants, 'Bind him hand and foot and cast him into the outer darkness. In that place there will be weeping and gnashing of teeth.' For many are called, but few are chosen."*

This passage initially seems so out of place. The king is basically inviting street people to the wedding and then is offended when one is not dressed up. It goes deeper than this. The wedding invitations broadened from Jews only to include Gentiles. But this does not mean they all just get "a free pass." By not dressing appropriately for the wedding would show no actions, no real faith.

James 2:17-18 gives an idea on the topic, *"So also faith by itself, if it does not have works, is dead. But someone will say, 'You have faith and I have works.' Show me your faith apart from your works, and I will show you my faith by my works."* Our faith should take action. However, it is not just that. Through Jesus Christ, we are clothed in righteousness.

Job 29:14 says, *"I put on righteousness, and it clothed me; my justice was like a robe and a turban."* Isaiah 61:10 adds, *"I will greatly rejoice in the LORD; my soul shall exult in my God, for he has clothed me with the garments of salvation; he has covered me with the robe of righteousness, as a bridegroom decks himself like a priest with a beautiful headdress, and as a bride adorns herself with her jewels."* Our actions reflect the heart. It is the walk and talk. We need to be clothed in His righteousness and then strive to be holy because He is holy.

Are you ready for the wedding?

What changes need to be made?

Black tie optional, but love, joy, peace, patience, kindness, goodness, faithfulness, gentleness, and self-control are preferred.

THE INVITATION: DEVOTION 3

EXCUSES

Dr. Randy T. Johnson | Growth Pastor

While being a pastor, I taught high school for 29 years and college for five. I have heard a number of excuses from students not having their homework done or being late to class. There was the usual, "My dog ate my homework," but with the technology, they have to blame the computer, printer, or claim an actual power outage. Excuses for being late for class consisted of "My mom did not wake me up," to blaming their alarm clock, being sick, traffic being bad, or caught by a train. I had students ask me to write a "doctor's note" for them. My favorite is the student who gave the excuse of "Fatigue and illness." When asked what was wrong, he said, "I am sick and tired of school." I always wondered if I was allowed to give a detention while laughing.

Luke 14:16-21 contains the parable of the banquet guests, *"But he said to him, "A man once gave a great banquet and invited many. And at the time for the banquet he sent his servant to say to those who had been invited, 'Come, for everything is now ready.' But they all alike began to make excuses. The first said to him, 'I have bought a field, and I must go out and see it. Please have me excused.' And another said, 'I have bought five yoke of oxen, and I go to examine them. Please have me excused.' And another said, 'I have married a wife, and therefore I cannot come.' So the servant came and reported these things to his master."*

The excuses abound. A guy buys a field and has to see it now? Another guy buys five yoke of oxen and has to check them now? Finally, a guy uses his new bride as an excuse. Is he putting the blame on her? The excuses are lame.

I heard a story of four boys who skipped morning classes to go fishing. On their way to class, they decided to give the excuse of a flat tire. When they got to school, all seemed to go well as the teacher did not challenge them. They sat down relieved. The teacher informed them that they needed a piece of paper and a pen because they missed a quiz but she was going to let them make it up. The quiz was only one question: Which tire was it?

Excuses are lies. Lies catch up with us. One of the problems with being a liar is you have to have a good memory. Another issue is how God views it.

Verse 21 gives the response of the master, **"Then the master of the house became angry and said to his servant, 'Go out quickly to the streets and lanes of the city, and bring in the poor and crippled and blind and lame.'"**

He was angry. They made lame excuses and flat out lied to him.

This reminds me of Luke 9:59, **"To another he said, 'Follow me.' But he said, 'Lord, let me first go and bury my father.'"** The excuse sounds legitimate until you realize his father is not dead. He does not want to disappoint his father and be disowned. He is not willing to forsake all and follow Jesus.

Excuses for not doing homework or being late for class are not life and death issues, but eternity is. There is not an excuse that will work before Jesus.

What excuses are you giving not to step out and follow Jesus more?

It is time to follow Jesus!

THE INVITATION: DEVOTION 4

WHOSOEVER

Dr. Randy T. Johnson | Growth Pastor

Luke 14:16-24 contains the parable of the Great Banquet, *"But he said to him, 'A man once gave a great banquet and invited many. And at the time for the banquet he sent his servant to say to those who had been invited, 'Come, for everything is now ready.' But they all alike began to make excuses. The first said to him, 'I have bought a field, and I must go out and see it. Please have me excused.' And another said, 'I have bought five yoke of oxen, and I go to examine them. Please have me excused.' And another said, 'I have married a wife, and therefore I cannot come.' So the servant came and reported these things to his master. Then the master of the house became angry and said to his servant, 'Go out quickly to the streets and lanes of the city, and bring in the poor and crippled and blind and lame.' And the servant said, 'Sir, what you commanded has been done, and still there is room.' And the master said to the servant, 'Go out to the highways and hedges and compel people to come in, that my house may be filled. For I tell you, none of those men who were invited shall taste my banquet.'"*

Our excuses can get us in trouble. They can label us and have us miss out on much more. It is comforting to know there is still room at the Great Banquet. An interesting aspect of this parable is the group known as *"the poor and crippled and blind and lame."* The audience hearing Jesus' words would have been caught off guard. They viewed this group as cursed by God because of sin.

Even the disciples thought this way. John 9:1-3 says, *"As he passed by, he saw a man blind from birth. And his disciples* asked him, 'Rabbi, who sinned, this man or his parents, that he was born blind?' Jesus answered, 'It was not that this man sinned, or his parents, but that the works of God might be displayed in him.'"* We are challenged to view this disadvantaged group differently.

Matthew 25:37-40 says, *"Then the righteous will answer him, saying, 'Lord, when did we see you hungry and feed you, or thirsty and give you drink? And when did we see you a stranger and welcome you, or naked and clothe you? And when did we see you sick or in prison and visit you?' And the King will answer them, 'Truly, I say to you, as you did it to one of the least of these my brothers, you did it to me.'"* When we help the hungry, sick, and even inmates, we serve Jesus.

James 1:27 takes it a step further, *"Religion that is pure and undefiled before God, the Father, is this: to visit orphans and widows in their affliction, and to keep oneself unstained from the world."* We need to help all without being judgmental. Love in action is the key. Loving God through loving people, especially individuals who can not repay the favor. It will then be pure and undefiled.

The Great Banquet is open to all. Come with your brokenness and be fixed.

Invite others!

THE INVITATION: DEVOTION 5

MESSIAH

Dr. Randy T. Johnson | Growth Pastor

I like sports. I typically enjoy watching college sports more than professional sports. Often a school or city will get excited at the arrival of a new star. I remember when Jason Kidd left college early to play pro basketball for the Dallas Mavericks. He said, "I am going to help this team make a 360-degree turn." He got teased. Did he mean he was going to help the team go from having a losing record to having a losing record? Maybe he should not have left college early. Seldom do these "saviors" bring a championship.

It is different with the Messiah. He is the "Anointed One." Messiah is the Hebrew word translated into Greek as Christ. He is the One especially appointed by God for His plan and purpose. His arrival was announced for thousands of years. He would be the true Savior.

Daniel 9:25 says, *"Know therefore and understand that from the going out of the word to restore and build Jerusalem to the coming of an anointed one, a prince, there shall be seven weeks. Then for sixty-two weeks it shall be built again with squares and moat, but in a troubled time."* Daniel speaks of the Anointed One and even calls Him a Prince. It was a familiar concept in the Old Testament. It was so common that even a pagan king knew that this Anointed One was coming. He tried to stop it by killing little boys.

This Anointed One, the Messiah, the Christ is listed in Matthew 1:16, *"And Jacob the father of Joseph the husband of Mary, of whom Jesus was born, who is called Christ."* This seemingly simple statement of Jesus being the Christ changed the world. It goes all the way back to man's first sin and hence the need for a Savior.

It should not surprise us that ordinary Jewish men who were not even scribes or scholars anticipated His arrival. John 1:41 says, **"He first found his own brother Simon and said to him, 'We have found the Messiah' (which means Christ)."**

In John 4 we find a woman who knows of the Messiah coming. Women did not get special training. Besides that she had many previous husbands and was living with a guy now. She would not have been respected by many. She was not described as holy. Verse 25 says, **"The woman said to him, 'I know that Messiah is coming (he who is called Christ). When he comes, he will tell us all things.'"**

I have to be careful about getting too excited over college football and basketball. The next great star might transfer, get injured, or leave early for the pros. It will pass and not make a difference in the world.

Only one "Superstar" came to change the world. There is something else different about Him. Mark 10:45 says, **"For even the Son of Man came not to be served but to serve, and to give his life as a ransom for many."** He avoided the limelight. He was humble. He came for others. He focused on others. It was not 'all about Him,' but to us it is 'all about Him.'

We need to receive Him, serve Him, serve others, and be ready for His return.

THE INVITATION: DEVOTION 6

THE LORD OUR RIGHTEOUSNESS

Dr. Randy T. Johnson | Growth Pastor

Do you struggle with the concept of "forgive and forget?" I write down everything. I am the king of the sticky note because the one thing I can remember is that I do not have a good memory. However, I can remember some of those times when I was hurt by someone else. Is it wrong that I do not forget? Can you truly forgive if you do not forget?

I think we would all agree that forgiveness is mandatory. C.S. Lewis said, "To be a Christian means to forgive the unexcusable because God has forgiven the inexcusable in you." We must forgive. However, I do not think we can force ourselves to forget something. I believe we must forgive and never use it against them again.

God is Jehovah-Tsidkenu, The Lord our Righteousness. We are forgiven because He imparts His righteousness to us. He covers us. God does not forget our sin; He chooses not to use it against us because He sees the Lord our Righteousness.

Jeremiah 23:5-6 boldly says, *"Behold, the days are coming, declares the LORD, when I will raise up for David a righteous Branch, and he shall reign as king and deal wisely, and shall execute justice and righteousness in the land. In his days Judah will be saved, and Israel will dwell securely. And this is the name by which he will be called: 'The LORD is our righteousness.'"* Jeremiah does not stop there as he says in 33:16, *"In those days Judah will be saved, and Jerusalem will dwell securely. And this is the name by which it will be called: 'The LORD is our righteousness.'"* It is not by our own works that we are saved. It is because of the work of The Lord our Righteousness.

2 Corinthians 5:21 states it clearly, **"For our sake he made him to be sin who knew no sin, so that in him we might become the righteousness of God."** Wow, we were born into sin, lived in sin, and deserved to die in sin with its consequence. However, Jesus, the perfect Son of God became sin for us so that we would be presented before God pure, clean, and righteous.

I would hear people say, "God forgives and forgets." How can God forget? If He forgets my sin that is great, but what if He forgets me? By definition, can God forget?

Micah 7:19 helped me, **"He will again have compassion on us; he will tread our iniquities underfoot. You will cast all our sins into the depths of the sea."** Scripture does not say that God will forget our sin. It says He throws it into the depths of the sea and then posts a sign that says, "No fishing."

God forgives. We need to forgive others, ourselves, and accept God's forgiveness. Learn from the past, but do not be held back. Press forward to the high calling of Jesus Christ.

Remember: No fishing allowed.

13

1988

Dr. Randy T. Johnson | Growth Pastor

In 1988 Angela and I were living in Cadillac with our two children. I was playing on the church's softball team. After the game, the other team gave us a booklet, "88 Reasons Why The Rapture Will Be In 1988." To cover the world time changes, the book said it would happen between September 11-13. Angela's birthday is September 15. I wrapped the book for her in case I "missed" her birthday. She did not appreciate my humor. Nothing happened on September 11-13, so I hurried and went birthday shopping and the author pushed and wrote, "89 Reasons Why The Rapture Will Be In 1989." Supposedly, Edgar Whisenant forgot to account for the year of the trumpets. Books followed in 1993 and then 1994. Whisenant was quoted as saying, "Only if the Bible is in error am I wrong; and I say that to every preacher in town."

Do you believe the Lord could return at any time? _____

_____
_____
_____

What do you want to accomplish before the Lord's return? _____

_____
_____
_____

In Matthew 24:32-44 Jesus uses a parable of a Fig Tree to convey His point, *"From the fig tree learn its lesson: as soon as its branch becomes tender and puts out its leaves, you know that summer is near. 33 So also, when you see all these things, you know that he is near, at the very gates. 34 Truly, I say to you, this generation will not pass away until all these things take place. 35 Heaven and earth will pass away, but my words will not pass away."*

What is your favorite season of the year? _____
_____
_____

What indicators is Jesus referring to as pointing that the time is near? _____
_____
_____

What does verse 35 mean? _____
_____
_____

36 "But concerning that day and hour no one knows, not even the angels of heaven, nor the Son, but the Father only. 37 For as were the days of Noah, so will be the coming of the Son of Man. 38 For as in those days before the flood they were eating and drinking, marrying and giving in marriage, until the day when Noah entered the ark, 39 and they were unaware until the flood came and swept them all away, so will be the coming of the Son of Man."

How is it possible that Jesus would not know the time of His return? _____
_____
_____

What characteristics were prevalent in the days of Noah? _____
_____
_____
_____

Do you see this same kind of generation today? _____
_____
_____
_____

40 Then two men will be in the field; one will be taken and one left. 41 Two women will be grinding at the mill; one will be taken and one left. 42 Therefore, stay awake, for you do not know on what day your Lord is coming. 43 But know this, that if the master of the house had known in what part of the night the thief was coming, he would have stayed awake and would not have let his house be broken into. 44 Therefore you also must be ready, for the Son of Man is coming at an hour you do not expect.

What does it mean to *"stay awake"* in verse 42? _____
_____
_____
_____

How is the analogy of a thief helpful? _____
_____
_____

What is Jesus stealing and from whom? _____
_____
_____
_____

How would you explain the Second Coming of Jesus to an unbeliever? _____
_____
_____

I was raised with a fear of "would you want to be doing that when Jesus comes?" Living in fear is not healthy. I should be active in my love for the Lord; therefore, when He returns, I will be ready.

Billy Graham said, "We are to wait for the coming of Christ with patience. We are to watch with anticipation. We are to work with Zeal. We are to prepare with urgency. Scripture says Christ is coming when you're least expecting him. Coming as a thief. He said, 'Be prepared. Get Ready. Prepare to meet thy God. Are you prepared?'"

1988: DEVOTION 1

"ARE YOU READY?"

Dr. Randy T. Johnson | Growth Pastor

"*From the fig tree learn its lesson: as soon as its branch becomes tender and puts out its leaves, you know that summer is near. So also, when you see these things taking place, you know that he is near, at the very gates. Truly, I say to you, this generation will not pass away until all these things take place. Heaven and earth will pass away, but my words will not pass away. But concerning that day or that hour, no one knows, not even the angels in heaven, nor the Son, but only the Father.*" (Mark 13:28-32)

Jesus is coming again! That is encouraging, but can also be a little scary. Well, maybe it is very scary. Many will be unprepared, empty handed, and without excuse. There is a poem entitled, "Are You Ready?" The author is unknown. Although he mixes the Return of Christ with the Last Judgment, I think this poem brings a nice change of pace and has a powerful message.

Twas the night before Jesus came and all through the house,
Not a creature was praying, not one in the house.
Their Bibles were lain on the shelf without care,
In hopes that Jesus would not come there.
The children were dressing to crawl into bed,
Not one ever kneeling or bowing a head.
And Mom in her rocker with baby on her lap,
Was watching the Late Show while I took a nap.
When out of the East there arose such a clatter,
I sprang to my feet to see what was the matter.
Away to the window I flew like a flash,
Tore open the shutters and threw up the sash!

When what to my wondering eyes should appear,
But angels proclaiming that Jesus was here.
With a light like the sun sending forth a bright ray,
I knew in a moment this must be THE DAY!
The light of His face made me cover my head,
It was Jesus returning just like He had said.
And though I possessed worldly wisdom and wealth,
I cried when I saw Him in spite of myself.
In the Book of Life which He held in His hand,
Was written the name of every saved man.
He spoke not a word as He searched for my name;
When He said "It's not here" my head hung in shame.
The people whose names had been written with love,
He gathered to take to His Father above.
With those who were ready He rose without a sound,
While all the rest were left standing around.
I fell to my knees, but it was too late,
I had waited too long and thus sealed my fate.
I stood and I cried as they rose out of sight;
Oh, if only I had been ready tonight.
In the words of this poem the meaning is clear,
The coming of Jesus is drawing near.
There's only one life and when comes the last call,
We'll find that the Bible was true after all!

Are you ready?

1988: DEVOTION 2

PUNXSUTAWNEY PHIL

Dr. Randy T. Johnson | Growth Pastor

"Red skies at night, sailors delight; red skies in the morning, sailors take warning." We have always looked for signs or indicators. If you are a sailor or just hoping to fish, you might want to look up. The skies can give a clue.

I remember my neighbor mentioning how it was going to be a rough winter. He was an old farm boy who said, "Look how fat the squirrels are. There are acorns everywhere. Watch the squirrels; they are stocking up."

We look for winter to come and to leave. My family celebrates Groundhog's Day. Every year on February 2nd we buy gifts, have a special dinner, and even have cake. By the way, our son was born on February 2nd. However, there are those in Punxsutawney, Pennsylvania who do take it seriously by dressing in black tie, with the top hat, waiting to see what "Phil" will do.

If we question Phil's instincts, then we can wait for early March, "Enter like a lion, leave like a lamb." We look for a sign of something to come.

Jesus used nature in His parable reminding us to see the signs of something to come. Luke 21:29-33 says, *"And he told them a parable: 'Look at the fig tree, and all the trees. As soon as they come out in leaf, you see for yourselves and know that the summer is already near. So also, when you see these things taking place, you know that the kingdom of God is near. Truly, I say to you, this generation will not pass away until all has taken place. Heaven and earth will*

pass away, but my words will not pass away.'" Jesus refers to trees and how they respond to the different seasons. We see trees and plants start budding in the Spring. Later we appreciate "the color change" as we drive by seeing trees that have changed from a green to bring orange, yellow, and even vibrant red. Then the trees "die" and lose all their leaves only to start the cycle again in the Spring. It gives a beautiful picture of death and resurrection, but Jesus uses it to warn us to be ready for some tough times coming. The times will get ugly, real ugly and then Jesus will return.

In commenting on Jesus' return, A.W. Tozer said, "If man had his way, the plan of redemption would be an endless and bloody conflict. In reality, salvation was bought not by Jesus' fist, but by His nail-pierced hands; not by muscle but by love; not by vengeance but by forgiveness; not by force but by sacrifice. Jesus Christ our Lord surrendered in order that He might win; He destroyed His enemies by dying for them and conquered death by allowing death to conquer Him."

Waiting for the Lord's return should not make us arrogant or vengeful. Some in the world think Christians are happy that unbelievers are going to Hell. I have heard some say that Christians thin they are better than everyone else because they are going to heaven. This is so sad. Tozer's quote spoke of love, forgiveness, and sacrifice. That should be our lot in life.

How will you show Jesus to others today?

1988: DEVOTION 3

DO NOT JUST LOOK BUSY

Dr. Randy T. Johnson | Growth Pastor

When I graduated from high school, my dad encouraged me to go door-to-door asking for a job. I was raised in an area by Detroit that had a lot of factories which supplied The Big 3. No one was hiring. First, I walked a mile in each direction going to each office asking if they had anything open. Next, I drove a mile away, parked my car, and started the adventure again. On Friday, I walked into an office and asked if they were hiring. I said I would work any hours, doing anything. The secretary paused as the man behind her started to speak. He was an older gentleman but was filthy. He said, "I can use some fresh muscle. Fill out this application." He then walked out. The secretary smiled, handed me an application, and said they were not hiring, but he was the owner. I filled everything out except what I expected to get paid. He came back in the room with another man who was covered in grease. He looked at the application and noticed I did not fill in that one section. He asked why I did not fill it in and I admitted that I did not know what minimum wage was. He informed me that I would not receive minimum wage. I said, "That is okay, I just need a job." He laughed and offered me about $2.00 an hour more. He asked when I could start. I said, "Tomorrow." He smiled and told me to enjoy the weekend and show up Monday morning at 6:30 am. I was shocked and asked how I should dress as I did not even know what I was going to do. He said, "See that man? Dress like that; you just took his job." It was an awkward moment.

The job went great. I ground the edges off of metal pieces to make them smooth for the welders. Within a few weeks my section went from being two weeks behind to two weeks ahead. One day Art, the owner, approached me. He said he had been watching me and was very pleased with my performance, but had a suggestion. He said that when I worked on the grinder, I often crossed my legs. It looked like I was not working hard, but he knew I was. So, he taught me how "to look busy." As he walked away, I thanked him and thought to myself, "Did the owner just show me how to look busy?"

Luke 12:42-48 gives the parable of a manager who makes a surprise visit on his servants, ***"And the Lord said, 'Who then is the faithful and wise manager, whom his master will set over his household, to give them their portion of food at the proper time? 43 Blessed is that servant whom his master will find so doing when he comes. 44 Truly, I say to you, he will set him over all his possessions. 45 But if that servant says to himself, 'My master is delayed in coming,' and begins to beat the male and female servants, and to eat and drink and get drunk, 46 the master of that servant will come on a day when he does not expect him and at an hour he does not know, and will cut him in pieces and put him with the unfaithful. 47 And that servant who knew his master's will but did not get ready or act according to his will, will receive a severe beating. 48 But the one who did not know, and did what deserved a beating, will receive a light beating. Everyone to whom much was given, of him much will be required, and from him to whom they entrusted much, they will demand the more.'"***

We all want to know what people are doing when we are gone. When we go out on date night with our spouse, we wonder what the babysitter is doing with and for our child. As the children get older and we leave for an overnight adventure, we wonder if they are safe and if they decided to have "a few" friends over. Will the house be trashed? Will I have to apologize to my neighbors? We worry at work that, "When the cat's away, the mice will play."

Should we do a surprise visit?

Jesus will. He is coming again. Are we ready?

The passage concludes with, ***"Everyone to whom much was given, of him much will be required."*** We know the truth. We are expected to step up. We do not need just to make sure we are ready; we need to help others. We need to warn them. Do not just look busy.

It is a life and death situation – forever.

1988: DEVOTION 4

PRAY FOR OUR CHILDREN

Dr. Randy T. Johnson | Growth Pastor

We need to pray for our children. This next generation has it tough. It seems each generation is getting more and more desensitized. What use to seem unthinkable is now landing somewhere between acceptable and expected. Unfortunately, we tend to compare ourselves with the world. If we are more conservative than others, we are godly. This is not godliness, at best it is morality.

I have heard people counsel, "Do not worry about your child, they will come back." They then go on to use the Prodigal or Lost Son as an illustration. That parable tells us that "if" they come back they will be welcomed by the Father." It does not guarantee they will come back.

We can not avoid the Parable of the Barren Fig Tree in Luke 13:6-9, *"And he told this parable: "A man had a fig tree planted in his vineyard, and he came seeking fruit on it and found none. And he said to the vinedresser, 'Look, for three years now I have come seeking fruit on this fig tree, and I find none. Cut it down. Why should it use up the ground?' And he answered him, 'Sir, let it alone this year also, until I dig around it and put on manure. Then if it should bear fruit next year, well and good; but if not, you can cut it down.'"* Fruit trees are expected to bear fruit. I know that does not sound too profound, but it is important to accept this concept. If they do not fulfill their purpose, then they are not needed. Would God cause someone to get sick to get their attention or even allow them to die since they are not producing? Is this found anywhere else in Scripture?

1 Corinthians 11:27-32 is a passage we read just about every time we participate in the Lord's Supper. It says, *"Whoever, therefore, eats the bread or drinks the cup of the Lord in an unworthy manner will be guilty concerning the body and blood of the Lord. Let a person examine himself, then, and so eat of the bread and drink of the cup. For anyone who eats and drinks without discerning the body eats and drinks judgment on himself. That is why many of you are weak and ill, and some have died. But if we judged ourselves truly, we would not be judged. But when we are judged by the Lord, we are disciplined so that we may not be condemned along with the world."* People were directly or inadvertently mocking the Lord's Supper. They missed the meaning. As a result, some were weak, ill, or even died.

I am not trying to put a dark cloud over your day. My goal is for us to pray. As we pray, we should examine our own lives. Are we active in the work of the Lord? Are we growing in the Lord? Is it clear we are a follower of Jesus? Then we should pray for our children. I daily pray that my kids will notice how active God is around them and give Him credit.

We need to pray for our children.

1988: DEVOTION 5

STRONGEST EVER

Dr. Randy T. Johnson | Growth Pastor

I have a friend who is debating on being a professional golf long drive competitor. His job would be to hit a golf ball as far as he can. He would travel all over the country and possibly into other parts of the world. His swing speed is about 150 mph and he can drive the ball over 400 yards. He is always breaking golf shafts and collapsing golf club heads. Fortunately, he has several sponsors. He has hundreds of clubs. Companies want him to use their brand. The goal is to find the strongest material, while yet light, in the world. Presently, there is a magnesium alloy. Companies are constantly looking for the best. We have gone from Steel to Titanium to Tungsten. It is a constant search. Strength is impressive.

Revelation 1:8 says, *"I am the Alpha and the Omega,' says the Lord God, 'who is and who was and who is to come, the Almighty.'"* Jesus is the Almighty. He is all-powerful. Nothing is beyond His reach or impossible for Him. He always has been and always will be. What He starts, He finishes.

Isaiah 9:6 describes baby Jesus and His characteristics, *"For to us a child is born, to us a son is given; and the government shall be upon his shoulder, and his name shall be called Wonderful Counselor, Mighty God, Everlasting Father, Prince of Peace."* It is interesting that Isaiah combines Jesus being "mighty" and still be peaceful. It is power under control. It is power with a purpose.

When life gets us done and we feel like we are being defeated, we need to praise God through Psalm 24:8, *"Who is this King of glory? The LORD, strong and mighty, the LORD, mighty in*

battle! He is the undisputed champion of the world. He will go into battle with us and for us. He wins!

Jesus is the King of kings and Lord of lords (1 Timothy 6:15). He is both the power of God and the wisdom of God (1 Corinthians 1:24).

I remember the silly argument between two elementary boys as they push each other, "My dad can beat up your dad." "No, he cannot. My dad is bigger than your dad." Eventually, they both run off to find their dads and prove their case. Fortunately, both parents just stayed home. However, our Dad is the strongest ever. He is the Almighty.

Nahum 1:3 paints a beautiful picture, ***"The LORD is slow to anger and great in power, and the LORD will by no means clear the guilty. His way is in whirlwind and storm, and the clouds are the dust of his feet."*** Picture Him standing on the clouds. He is majestic. He is the Almighty.

No challenge is too big for Him. No relationship is too broken for Him. No addiction is too consuming for Him. At the same time, no request is too small for Him.

He is the Lord Almighty.

1988: DEVOTION 6

GOD EVERLASTING

Dr. Randy T. Johnson | Growth Pastor

The Energizer Bunny. What thoughts come to mind? You have that little pink bunny playing his drum as he scoots across the screen. "He just keeps going and going and..." For almost 30 years he has been the "face" of Energizer batteries. He symbolizes a significant length of time. He is the Energizer Bunny.

Psalm 90:1-2 also refer to a length of time, *"Lord, you have been our dwelling place in all generations. Before the mountains were brought forth, or ever you had formed the earth and the world, from everlasting to everlasting you are God."* He is the beginning and the end, the one who works His purposes throughout the ages.

Abraham used an unusual name for God in Genesis 21:33, *"Abraham planted a tamarisk tree in Beersheba and called there on the name of the LORD, the Everlasting God."* He is El Olam. He is the Eternal God. He is the Everlasting God. Abraham called out to the Eternal God knowing He gives strength to the weary.

Isaiah 40:28 continues the thought, *"Have you not known? Have you not heard? The LORD is the everlasting God, the Creator of the ends of the earth. He does not faint or grow weary; his understanding is unsearchable."* God always was and will always be. He is not slowing down.

How could God have always been? That is a tough question. I am reminded of a story Reverend Martin Dale shared, "I remember Billy Graham going on French television and being told by the commentator: 'Dr. Graham, you have two minutes to prove to us God exists.' To which Billy Graham replied: 'I can't do that but I can tell you what I do know: For God so loved the world that he gave his only begotten Son that whoever believes in him will not perish but have everlasting life.'"

I cannot explain everything like gravity, wind, and an Everlasting God. I cannot see them, but I do feel their power. I see the effect and working they accomplish.

I want to close this devotion with the lyrics (by Brenton Brown and Ken Riley) for the song, Everlasting God.
Strength will rise as we wait upon the Lord
We will wait upon the Lord
We will wait upon the Lord

Strength will rise as we wait upon the Lord
We will wait upon the Lord
We will wait upon the Lord
Our God, You reign forever
Our Hope, our strong Deliverer

You are the everlasting God
The everlasting God
You do not faint; You won't grow weary
You're the defender of the weak
You comfort those in need
You lift us up on wings like eagles

Amen.

14

GOT OIL?

Dr. Randy T. Johnson | Growth Pastor

The Girl Scout motto is "Be prepared." In the 1947 *Girl Scout Handbook*, the motto was explained this way, "A Girl Scout is ready to help out wherever she is needed. Willingness to serve is not enough; you must know how to do the job well, even in an emergency."

To "Be prepared" is a common theme in Scripture, too. The original audience for the parables was Jewish, but they have great application for everyone. We need to be prepared. Part of being prepared is to be on time. One of my professors, Howard Hendricks, said everyone is punctual. Maybe, punctually five minutes late, but they are always five minutes late. It becomes a habitual habit.

Are you typically five minutes early, right on time, or five minutes late for most things? _____
_____
_____

Do you tend to have everything you need, not enough, or too much?
_____
_____
_____

Matthew 25:1-13 presents the parable of ten virgins waiting for the groom. Some were ready; some were not.

"Then the kingdom of heaven will be like ten virgins who took their lamps and went to meet the bridegroom. 2 Five of them were foolish, and five were wise."

What is the Kingdom of Heaven? _____
_____
_____

The Church is referred to as Christ's virgin in 2 Corinthians 11:2 ***"For I feel a divine jealousy for you, since I betrothed you to one husband, to present you as a pure virgin to Christ."***

How could that relate here? _____
_____
_____

"For when the foolish took their lamps, they took no oil with them, 4 but the wise took flasks of oil with their lamps."

How are the young girls in the parable similar? _____
_____
_____
_____

How are the young girls in the parable different from each other?
_____
_____
_____

"As the bridegroom was delayed, they all became drowsy and slept."

What would cause "The Bridegroom" to be delayed? _____
_____
_____
_____

"But at midnight there was a cry, 'Here is the bridegroom! Come out to meet him.' 7 Then all those virgins rose and trimmed their lamps. 8 And the foolish said to the wise, 'Give us some of your oil, for our lamps are going out.'"

Why would the wise virgins not give up some of their oil? _____
_____
_____
_____

When are there times when a Christian should not share or give in? _____
_____
_____

"But the wise answered, saying, 'Since there will not be enough for us and for you, go rather to the dealers and buy for yourselves.' 10 And while they were going to buy, the bridegroom came, and those who were ready went in with him to the marriage feast, and the door was shut."

How do you feel about the door being shut? _____
_____
_____
_____

"Afterward the other virgins came also, saying, 'Lord, lord, open to us.' 12 But he answered, 'Truly, I say to you, I do not know you.' 13 Watch therefore, for you know neither the day nor the hour."

Does this parable end too harsh? _____
_____
_____

A few final thoughts:

1. Oil is often used to symbolize the Holy Spirit in Scripture. How could that relate to this parable? _____
_____
_____

2. How could 1 John 5:11-12 *("And this is the testimony, that God gave us eternal life, and this life is in his Son. 12 Whoever has the Son has life; whoever does not have the Son of God does not have life.")* summarize this parable? _____
_____
_____

3. How does 1 Peter 3:15 *("But in your hearts honor Christ the Lord as holy, always being prepared to make a defense to anyone who asks you for a reason for the hope that is in you; yet do it with gentleness and respect.")* relate to the topic of being prepared? _____
_____
_____

Bonus thought:

How do I answer the person who says, "I will wait for the 'rapture.' If I see everyone gone, then I will get saved?" _____

_____
_____
_____

2 Thessalonians 2:11-12 speaks of what will happen after the return of the Lord, **"Therefore God sends them a strong delusion, so that they may believe what is false, in order that all may be condemned who did not believe the truth but had pleasure in unrighteousness."**

Finally, how does the title "Got Oil?" relate to this parable?
_____
_____
_____

GOT OIL?: DEVOTION 1

A WALK DOWN 8 MILE

Dr. Randy T. Johnson | Growth Pastor

In college I drove a beautiful Honda 750. It was red with gold and black trim. The helmets matched the bike which was fully dressed out. It was fabulous. One day I was driving down 8 Mile and my bike just "died" on me. I had nothing. The gas gauge showed I had plenty of fuel, but I still checked the tank just in case. That was not the problem. Back then cell phones were not an option, and I could not just leave it for later (remember I am on 8 Mile), so I started walking while pushing this beast. A couple of different people stopped and asked if I ran out of gas. I replied, "No, I am not sure what is wrong." Finally, one guy pulled over and stopped. He asked if I had checked the fuses. I must admit, I did not know what he was talking about. He popped open the side panel and pulled off a fuse. "Yeap, you have a bad fuse. Hey, look here. There is a spare in this container." He put the fuse in and the bike started right up with no problem. Obviously, I was thrilled and thanked him. I immediately went and got another fuse in case I needed it in the future. It cost 25 cents. Amazing how much little things matter. I also appreciated how prepared the previous owner was to have another fuse. I would be prepared for the future.

Matthew 25:1-13 contains the parable of some young ladies being prepared and others not, *"Then the kingdom of heaven will be like ten virgins who took their lamps and went to meet the bridegroom. Five of them were foolish, and five were wise. For when the foolish took their lamps, they took no oil with them, but the wise took flasks of oil with their lamps. As the bridegroom was delayed, they all became drowsy and slept. But at midnight there was a cry, 'Here is the bridegroom! Come out to meet him.' Then all those virgins rose and trimmed their lamps. And the foolish said to the wise, 'Give us some of your oil, for our lamps are going out.' But the wise answered, saying, 'Since there will not be enough for us and for you, go rather to the dealers and buy for yourselves.' And while they were going to buy, the bridegroom came, and those who were ready went in with him to the marriage feast, and the door was shut. Afterward the other virgins came also, saying, 'Lord, lord, open to us.' But he answered, 'Truly, I say to you, I do not know you.' Watch therefore, for you know neither the day nor the hour."*

The Lord is coming again and we need to be prepared. 1 Thessalonians 4:14-18 say, *"For since we believe that Jesus died and rose again, even so, through Jesus, God will bring with him those who have fallen asleep. For this we declare to you by a word from the Lord, that we who are alive, who are left until the coming of the Lord, will not precede those who have fallen asleep. For the Lord himself will descend from heaven with a cry of command, with the voice of an archangel, and with the sound of the trumpet of God. And the dead in Christ will rise first. Then we who are alive, who are left, will be caught up together with them in the clouds to meet the Lord in the air, and so we will always be with the Lord. Therefore encourage one another with these words."*

I just want to point out a couple of things. One, it is evident from this passage that Jesus is coming again. Two, where Matthew reminds us to be ready, this passage uses the Return of the Lord as a means of encouragement.

Be ready. Be thankful. Be active in witnessing.

GOT OIL?: DEVOTION 2

THE AISLE

Dr. Randy T. Johnson | Growth Pastor

Weddings are for women. I have officiated at several weddings and it is interesting to talk to the couple in counseling or at dress rehearsal. There are some men who think the wedding is about them. I have even had to remind both moms that it was not their wedding. The focus is on the bride. She buys a dress; he typically rents a tuxedo. She has a whole bouquet of flowers and he might have one flower on his boutonniere. She dazzles and he is the sidekick. Should we talk about the price of their rings? The wedding is her's.

I tried to figure out the history of the woman walking down the aisle. The closest thing I could find was that her father brought her to her future husband with a dowry or price. Sounds sad, "I will pay you to take my daughter." Looking at Matthew 15 again, we see a different process.

"Then the kingdom of heaven will be like ten virgins who took their lamps and went to meet the bridegroom. Five of them were foolish, and five were wise. For when the foolish took their lamps, they took no oil with them, but the wise took flasks of oil with their lamps. As the bridegroom was delayed, they all became drowsy and slept. But at midnight there was a cry, 'Here is the bridegroom! Come out to meet him.' Then all those virgins rose and trimmed their lamps. And the foolish said to the wise, 'Give us some of your oil, for our lamps are going out.' But the wise answered, saying, 'Since there will not be enough for us and for you, go rather to the dealers and buy for yourselves.' And while they were going to buy, the bridegroom came, and those who were ready went in with him to the marriage feast, and the door

was shut. Afterward the other virgins came also, saying, 'Lord, lord, open to us.' But he answered, 'Truly, I say to you, I do not know you.' Watch therefore, for you know neither the day nor the hour." Matthew 25:1-13

Jesus is coming back. Jesus, the Bridegroom, comes down the aisle to take His bride, the Church. Jesus, the man, walks down the aisle. I have mentioned to a few couples that it would make more sense if the man came down the aisle. Typically, they say, "That's interesting." However, you and I know she is practicing her steps as she comes down the aisle. She is focusing on not stepping on her dress. So, she will smile, hold her head up high, and slowly walk down the aisle to "receive" her groom.

The next time you are at a wedding, take a moment to remember that Jesus is coming back for His Bride, the Church. He is coming back for us. That will be a time of celebration.

GOT OIL?: DEVOTION 3

EYES WIDE OPEN

Dr. Randy T. Johnson | Growth Pastor

While I was in Seminary, I worked full-time as a Security Officer. It was official stuff. We wore suit and tie. It was a beautiful structure that had two 25-story office towers that were connected with a mall, parking structure, and 5-star restaurant. In the center was an ice skating rink with a glass dome covering the structure. I worked midnight shift at their office tower that was connected by a skywalk.

It was a great job. I studied all night. They loved it because it meant I was awake. Also, being a seminary student helped them trust me. One night, right after I finished one of the rounds, I went into a plush office and sat on a fabulous couch. No one was around. It was about 4:00 am. I turned up my radio and closed my eyes for "a minute." You probably know where this is going. About an hour later, I checked my radio and had turned it down, not up. I jumped up and listened as the supervisor was calling me. His voice was a little stressed. I went down to the lobby. He said, "We have been looking for you for over half an hour." I apologized and said, "I fell asleep." He said, "You took the last round of checkpoints real slow?" I said, "No, I fell asleep." I was a little slow and did not catch on. Let's blame the lack of sleep. He smiled and said, "I am sure all your future rounds will be quicker." I thanked him.

It is embarrassing to get caught sleeping. Mark 13:33-37 gives a parable that emphasizes this point, ***"Be on guard, keep awake. For you do not know when the time will come. It is like a man going on a journey, when he leaves home and puts his servants in charge, each with his work, and commands the doorkeeper to stay awake. Therefore stay awake—for you*** *do not know when the master of the house will come, in the evening, or at midnight, or when the rooster crows, or in the morning— lest he come suddenly and find you asleep. And what I say to you I say to all: Stay awake."*

We need to stay awake. It is a common theme in sports. In baseball, when a player gets picked off a base, they say he got caught sleeping. In football, a defensive player can be caught off guard when the team throws a bomb after several running plays or on a fake punt. In basketball, you try to find the team sleeping and hit a backdoor pass. These are only sports and have no real lasting importance. Remember basketball player Eric "Sleepy" Floyd got the nickname from playing baseball as a kid.

However, we need to stay awake in other areas. We need to evaluate our own life. Are we ready for the return of the Master?

Next, we need to protect our family. We cannot let people sneak into our house through the door, window, TV, or internet. We need to be on guard. We need to help them be ready.

This can spread to our church. Let's make sure we stay focused on Jesus.

Be on the watch. Stay awake.

Horrible things are going to happen, but "not on my watch!"

GOT OIL?: DEVOTION 4

"READY OR NOT..."

Dr. Randy T. Johnson | Growth Pastor

"Ready or not, here I come." Do you remember playing hide-n-seek? I love watching children play this game. You start by counting to whatever number and then scream out that key phrase of warning. There are classic stories of hiding places, but the best is the child who still lives under the assumption that if I cannot see you, then you cannot see me. It is precious. I must confess I had played the game with my own children when I needed a break. Let's say I counted to something like 5,000 and then casually took a walk. Oh yeah, I did say, "Ready or not, here I come."

Luke 12:35-40 gives another parable on being ready for the return of the Lord. *"Stay dressed for action and keep your lamps burning, and be like men who are waiting for their master to come home from the wedding feast, so that they may open the door to him at once when he comes and knocks. Blessed are those servants whom the master finds awake when he comes. Truly, I say to you, he will dress himself for service and have them recline at table, and he will come and serve them. If he comes in the second watch, or in the third, and finds them awake, blessed are those servants! But know this, that if the master of the house had known at what hour the thief was coming, he would not have left his house to be broken into. You also must be ready, for the Son of Man is coming at an hour you do not expect."*

We need to be dressed ready for His surprise arrival. In this parable the man is dressed for service. Being clothed in righteousness is a common theme in Scripture.

Revelation 3:4 says, *"Yet you have still a few names in Sardis, people who have not soiled their garments, and they will walk with me in white, for they are worthy."* By saying some have not soiled their garments implies many have. We need to have a walk symbolized as pure white.

If our garments are soiled, we need to ask forgiveness. Zechariah 3:4 says, *"And the angel said to those who were standing before him, 'Remove the filthy garments from him.' And to him he said, 'Behold, I have taken your iniquity away from you, and I will clothe you with pure vestments.'"*

As Jesus said to the woman caught in adultery, "Go and sin no more." We are forgiven and God has removed our filthy garments and dressed us in purity.

Isaiah 61:10 continues the thought, *"I will greatly rejoice in the LORD; my soul shall exult in my God, for he has clothed me with the garments of salvation; he has covered me with the robe of righteousness, as a bridegroom decks himself like a priest with a beautiful headdress, and as a bride adorns herself with her jewels."* Again, we have a robe of righteousness. We need to be holy for He is holy. Our walk matters. It is part of being ready.

Job 29:14 says, *"I put on righteousness, and it clothed me; my justice was like a robe and a turban."*

Jesus warned, "Ready or not, here I come." He is on His way. We need to be clothed with the garments of salvation along with the robe of righteousness.

GOT OIL?: DEVOTION 5

BRIDEGROOM

Dr. Randy T. Johnson | Growth Pastor

Little girls often love to play house and even the wedding ceremony. I remember as kids mocking, "Here comes the bride, all dressed in pink; open the windows, and let out the stink." The second chorus involved me running. However, we as a Church are a mess and do stink the place up at times, but the Groom has made us white as snow. Therefore, "Here comes the bride, all dressed in white; none can compare to her beautiful site."

Jesus is the Bridegroom. He is coming back for His Bride, the Church. He will lead her and care for her.

In Matthew 9:15 Jesus refers to himself as the Bridegroom, *"And Jesus said to them, 'Can the wedding guests mourn as long as the bridegroom is with them? The days will come when the bridegroom is taken away from them, and then they will fast.'"* Jesus knows His position and mission.

John 3:29 continues the concept, *"The one who has the bride is the bridegroom. The friend of the bridegroom, who stands and hears him, rejoices greatly at the bridegroom's voice. Therefore this joy of mine is now complete."* We as the Bride, listen for His voice. We are comforted by His tone. We are secure in His love.

Revelation 21:9 refers to the Groom as the Lamb, which is Jesus, *"Then came one of the seven angels who had the seven bowls full of the seven last plagues and spoke to me, saying, 'Come, I will show you the Bride, the wife of the Lamb.'"* It is an exciting time of the ceremony when I get to "introduce" the couple to the assembly. I will often place emphasis in my words, "It is now my privilege to introduce Mr. and 'the Mrs.' Jesus Christ."

A husband has responsibilities. First, he is to be a leader. He is to think past today. He needs to have a plan. Second, he needs to love his wife. This unconditional love does not always come naturally, but it is his job. Third, he is to provide for her. Finances are involved, but there is more to it. He is to provide for her emotionally, physically, and spiritually. Finally, he is to serve her. Leadership is shown best in service. Love is shown in action.

Think of Jesus. He makes for a great husband. He is the Groom. He told us He is coming. A yes to His proposal means taking Him as husband. It means being the Church. It means following His leadership. A yes involves being ready for whenever He returns.

Maybe the Wedding March should go something like:
Here comes the Groom
All dressed in light,
Are you ready?
For day or night?

GOT OIL?: DEVOTION 6

GOT YOUR BACK

Dr. Randy T. Johnson | Growth Pastor

I remember as a kid when a couple of friends and I were getting bullied by another guy. I finally said to the guys that we needed to team up and take him down. They agreed and we called him out and started toward him. As I boldly got closer, I felt an empty feeling. I turned my shoulder to be encouraged by my buddies only to find out they deserted me. I ran. I did not have to outrun the bully, only one of my friends.

We all have experienced that moment or time when we feel all alone. That is when we need to remember Jehovah-Shammah. It is the name that means the Lord is There or the Lord my Companion. God's presence is not limited or contained in the tabernacle or temple. The veil has been torn wide open. He is accessible to all who love and obey Him.

Ezekiel 48:35 uses this particular name concerning God, *"The circumference of the city shall be 18,000 cubits. And the name of the city from that time on shall be, The LORD Is There."* God is there. That brings such comfort.

Most people are familiar with the start of Psalm 46:10, *"Be still, and know that I am God."* It becomes even more meaningful when we see the rest of the chapter. Verses 1-3 start by saying, *"God is our refuge and strength, a very present help in trouble. Therefore we will not fear though the earth gives way, though the mountains be moved into the heart of the sea, though its waters roar and foam, though the mountains tremble at its swelling. Selah."* Even though our world is shaking all around us, we know God is, *"a very present help in trouble."* Verse 7 continues the thought, *"The LORD of hosts is with us; the God of Jacob is our fortress. Selah."* Finally the chapter ends saying, *"The LORD of hosts is with us; the God of Jacob is our fortress. Selah."* We can be still because we know He is God and He is very present with us.

Jesus promises in Matthew 28:19-20 to be with us, *"Go therefore and make disciples of all nations, baptizing them in the name of the Father and of the Son and of the Holy Spirit, teaching them to observe all that I have commanded you. And behold, I am with you always, to the end of the age."*

It is hard when we feel we are all alone. Paul shares the emotions in 2 Timothy 4:16-17, *"At my first defense no one came to stand by me, but all deserted me. May it not be charged against them! But the Lord stood by me and strengthened me, so that through me the message might be fully proclaimed and all the Gentiles might hear it. So I was rescued from the lion's mouth."* I understand people giving Paul distance as he has a habit of getting beat up and thrown in prison. He was alone – well kind of. God was with him and he knew it.

I remember as a teen hearing Eric Carmen sing, "All by Myself." The chorus goes, "All by myself. Don't want to be all by myself anymore. All by myself. Don't want to live all by myself anymore." We do not have to be all alone. We can seek out God and find He is a very present help.

Proverbs 18:24 says it so well, *"A man of many companions may come to ruin, but there is a friend who sticks closer than a brother."*

Do you know that friend? He created you and has chosen to stay nearby.

15

1 + 0 = 0

Dr. Randy T. Johnson | Growth Pastor

Matthew 25:14-30 tells the Parable of the Talents. Hall of Fames basketball player Larry Bird said, "A winner is someone who recognizes his God-given talents, works his tail off to develop them into skills, and uses these skills to accomplish his goals." I agree with this quote if we change one letter from "his goals" to "His goals." This parable is very well-known but possibly misinterpreted. It should bring some deep thoughts, open discussion, and challenging applications.

The central question that needs to come from the parable is whether Jesus is talking about rewards for service or salvation by grace. Is Jesus speaking to believers who need to get more involved or unbelievers who need to be ready for His return? There is always one interpretation, but several applications. This lesson will help distinguish those.

The world has a way of labeling or categorizing us. I remember running into one of my high school teachers who I had not seen in over 20 years. I introduced myself, and he said, "Johnson. Baptist. Baseball player." I was impressed with his memory and thankful for what he remembered.

What were you "known for" when you were younger (size, ability, personality, awards…)? _____
_____
_____

"For it will be like a man going on a journey, who called his servants and entrusted to them his property."

Have you ever had a house sitter or pet sitter? How did it go?
_____
_____
_____

Why is the master entrusting these servants? _____
_____
_____
_____

"To one he gave five talents, to another two, to another one, to each according to his ability. Then he went away."

A talent was either silver or gold and weighed between 58-80 pounds. The discussion here is about money, not abilities. However, abilities can be part of the application of this parable.

If someone gave you a million dollars, but wanted it back in 10 years, what would you do with it? _____
_____
_____

What emotions were probably present with each servant as he received his amount? _____
_____
_____

"He who had received the five talents went at once and traded with them, and he made five talents more. 17 So also he who had the two talents made two talents more. But he who had received the one talent went and dug in the ground and hid his master's money."

1 Corinthians 4:2 says, *"Moreover, it is required of stewards that they be found faithful."* Does this verse relate? _____
_____
_____
_____

Which servant's action surprised you most? _____
_____
_____
_____

"Now after a long time the master of those servants came and settled accounts with them."

What items do we talk about when we see someone we have not seen in a long time? _____
_____
_____

("Behold, I am coming soon, bringing my recompense with me, to repay each one for what he has done." Revelation 22:12)

"And he who had received the five talents came forward, bringing five talents more, saying, 'Master, you delivered to me five talents; here, I have made five talents more.' 21 His master said to him, 'Well done, good and faithful servant.

You have been faithful over a little; I will set you over much. Enter into the joy of your master.'"

Who should get the extra five talents? _____
_____
_____

How does the Master's response affect you? _____
_____
_____

What responses in your life were very meaningful? _____
_____
_____

"And he also who had the two talents came forward, saying, 'Master, you delivered to me two talents; here, I have made two talents more.' 23 His master said to him, 'Well done, good and faithful servant. You have been faithful over a little; I will set you over much. Enter into the joy of your master.'"

How is the response different between the servant with five talents and the servant with two? Why? _____
_____
_____

"He also who had received the one talent came forward, saying, 'Master, I knew you to be a hard man, reaping where you did not sow, and gathering where you scattered no seed, 25 so I was afraid, and I went and hid your talent in the ground. Here, you have what is yours.'"

Who does the third servant blame? How? _____
_____
_____
_____

What relationship do you think each servant had with the master?
_____
_____
_____

Does relationship make a difference? _____
_____
_____

"But his master answered him, 'You wicked and slothful servant! You knew that I reap where I have not sown and gather where I scattered no seed? 27 Then you ought to have invested my money with the bankers, and at my coming I should have received what was my own with interest.'"

How is the master like and unlike God? _____
_____
_____

"Hide not your talents, they for use were made. What's a sundial in the shade?" Benjamin Franklin

"So take the talent from him and give it to him who has the ten talents. 29 For to everyone who has will more be given, and he will have an abundance. But from the one who has not, even what he has will be taken away."

How does this relate to us today? _____
_____
_____

"And cast the worthless servant into the outer darkness. In that place there will be weeping and gnashing of teeth."

What place is referred to here? _____
_____
_____

How is the word ***"worthless"*** appropriate here? _____
_____
_____
_____

What "talents" or "resources" have we been given to further the Kingdom of God? _____
_____
_____

How does relationship with the Master make a difference?
_____
_____
_____

"Inside every human being there are treasures to unlock." Mike Huckabee

1 + 0 = 0: DEVOTION 1

IT'S ALL CHINESE TO ME

Dr. Randy T. Johnson | Growth Pastor

When I was in college, my Greek professor asked to speak with me. He informed me that he was pastoring the Chinese Bible Church of Detroit and asked if I would pray about being his Youth Minister while finishing my last two years of college. To be honest, one of my first thoughts was that I might finally be taller than most people at church. Obviously, that is a faulty stereotype as two of the elders had boys well over six feet tall. My main thought was on how special of an opportunity this would be, so I gladly took the position. Angela and I taught the youth Sunday School class, ran children's church, and then had a discipleship class after lunch for high school and college age. It was incredible. We thoroughly enjoyed it. We embraced the culture and they embraced us. I was able to put my schooling into use immediately. I felt blessed.

Right before college graduation, I was told the president of the college wanted to see me. I was nervous. I could not think of anything that I did wrong. He welcomed me into his office and asked how I was doing. He was very friendly and personable. He said he heard I was going on to Dallas Theological Seminary and congratulated me. Then came the reason for the meeting. He handed me an application for a full tuition scholarship for four years. He informed me he was chairman of the scholarship committee and that he was happy to help me. I was blown away. I did not have the money for school, but knew I was supposed to go.

As I look back, I believe the president and professor watched me be faithful in "little things" and believed I would be faithful at the next level. I never viewed the position as lesser and I have even helped three other Chinese Bible Churches start in the Detroit area.

Matthew 25 records the parable of the talents. If you remember, servants are given 5, 2, and one talent. The first two servants double their amount while the third servant buries his. Verses 19-21 record the response of the master to the first servant, **"Now after a long time the master of those servants came and settled accounts with them. And he who had received the five talents came forward, bringing five talents more, saying, 'Master, you delivered to me five talents; here, I have made five talents more.' His master said to him, 'Well done, good and faithful servant. You have been faithful over a little; I will set you over much. Enter into the joy of your master.'"** This displays such a beautiful picture. The master expresses his approval and elevates the servant's influence. For most of us the words would have been enough.

Are you going through an empty stage of life? Do you feel like you are taken for granted or overlooked? Remember it may just be a test to see if you would be faithful with more responsibility. Faithfulness is the key. Amy Carmichael makes an interesting point, "There have been times of late when I have had to hold on to one text with all my might: 'It is required in stewards that a man may be found faithful.' Praise God; it does not say 'successful.'"

Be faithful.

1 + 0 = 0: DEVOTION 2

"I CAN" OPENER

Dr. Randy T. Johnson | Growth Pastor

One year coaching golf, I gave all the boys a hand held can opener. I did not say anything and let them think about it over the weekend. At Monday's practice we talked about it. I took them to Philippians 4:13 which says, *"I can do all things through him who strengthens me."* I told them that the next round they lost a golf ball and had to reach into their golf bag, I wanted them to see the can opener and change their mindset from "I cannot" to "I can." It is an "I can" opener. They laughed and mocked me. Later in the season, one of the boys was having a rough round and saw the "dumb" can opener. He laughed to himself and he says it changed his round. We were tied with two tough opponents for the win. His score broke the tie and gave us the win. Some eight years later, at his wedding reception, he told me he still had the can opener.

Positive words can go a long way. Matthew 25:19-21 records the most positive words that could ever be stated, *"Now after a long time the master of those servants came and settled accounts with them. And he who had received the five talents came forward, bringing five talents more, saying, 'Master, you delivered to me five talents; here, I have made five talents more.' His master said to him, 'Well done, good and faithful servant. You have been faithful over a little; I will set you over much. Enter into the joy of your master.'"* Believers will often state how they long for the day when they will hear, *"Well done, good and faithful servant."*

We need to realize the power we have to make a difference for Christ. We can do all things through Him. A little shepherd boy did not just take on a giant one day, but every day walked with confidence. He took down a bear and a lion. He daily stepped forward. He took on new challenges. He was not a coward; he did not back down.

Eleanor Roosevelt said, "You must do the thing you think you cannot do." People have said, "God will not give you more than you can handle." This is a myth. He may give us more so that we are pushed to include Him. We need to realize our dependence on Him. I have taken on several projects that I could not do, knowing He would have to show up. He did.

What challenge has God placed before you? Think "I can" and step forward with the strength of the Lord. Remember the return on your investment is so meaningful in hearing The Master say, ***"Well done, good and faithful servant."***

1 + 0 = 0: DEVOTION 3
BLAME GAME
Dr. Randy T. Johnson | Growth Pastor

In Luke 19 we have a parable similar to that of the talents. It talks about a nobleman who needed to leave for a while to receive a kingdom. Before he left, he called together ten of his servants and gave each the same amount, ten minas. He told them to continue with business until he returned. Even though each received one mona, their performance differed. One servant brought a tenfold profit while another brought fivefold. The nobleman expressed his appreciation and pleasure to both.

However, another servant just came back with the one mina. Verses 20-24 record the situation, *"Then another came, saying, 'Lord, here is your mina, which I kept laid away in a handkerchief; for I was afraid of you, because you are a severe man. You take what you did not deposit, and reap what you did not sow.' He said to him, 'I will condemn you with your own words, you wicked servant! You knew that I was a severe man, taking what I did not deposit and reaping what I did not sow? Why then did you not put my money in the bank, and at my coming I might have collected it with interest?' And he said to those who stood by, 'Take the mina from him, and give it to the one who has the ten minas.'"* The servant blamed the nobleman for his laziness. It is not like he tried, but the market was bad. He did nothing. He put more energy into blaming his master than he did in investing the money.

In Genesis 3 we have the sin of Adam and Eve. After they sin, they hide from God. That sounds kind of funny. God finds them and asks what the problem was. They avoid the topic. He then asks if they disobeyed Him and ate from the tree. Genesis 3:12-13 gives their response, *"The man said, 'The woman whom you gave to be with me, she gave me fruit of the tree, and I ate.' Then the LORD God said to the woman, 'What is this that you have done?' The woman said, 'The serpent deceived me, and I ate.'"* Most people point out the natural chain reaction. The man blames the woman and the woman blames the serpent. However, it is worse than that. The man blames the woman, *'whom you gave to be with me."* In essence the man, Adam, blames God.

The blame game does not have a happy ending. We need to take ownership of out actions. Adam needed to man-up. We need to do the same.

My cousin, Terry, and I grew up as next door neighbors. He is like a big brother to me. I remember a speech he gave at his parents' 40th-anniversary family party. He said, "If you see anything good in me, give my parents credit. Anything bad you see in me, is my fault." That was so refreshing. So many people want to blame their parents well into their adulthood. They may have been horrible, but God intended for us to have them for a reason. We need to move on.

Thank God for your past. Use it to encourage others. Press on.

1 + 0 = 0: DEVOTION 4

ESCAR-GO-T

Dr. Randy T. Johnson | Growth Pastor

"**B**y perseverance the snail reached the ark." Charles Spurgeon

Luke 11:5-13 records a unique parable, *"And he said to them, 'Which of you who has a friend will go to him at midnight and say to him, 'Friend, lend me three loaves, for a friend of mine has arrived on a journey, and I have nothing to set before him'; and he will answer from within, 'Do not bother me; the door is now shut, and my children are with me in bed. I cannot get up and give you anything'? I tell you, though he will not get up and give him anything because he is his friend, yet because of his impudence he will rise and give him whatever he needs. And I tell you, ask, and it will be given to you; seek, and you will find; knock, and it will be opened to you. For everyone who asks receives, and the one who seeks finds, and to the one who knocks it will be opened. What father among you, if his son asks for a fish, will instead of a fish give him a serpent; or if he asks for an egg, will give him a scorpion? If you then, who are evil, know how to give good gifts to your children, how much more will the heavenly Father give the Holy Spirit to those who ask him!"*

This parable starts with a concept of being persistent. I found a survey by the National Retail Dry Goods Association fascinating. It says that 48% of the salesmen made one call and quit. Another 25% made two calls and quit. 15% made three calls and quit. So, 88% of the salesmen stopped before the fourth call. That makes sense, but the interesting point is that the other 12% of the agents who kept calling did 80% of the business. Persistence can pay off. We cannot quit.

Our persistence should start with our own salvation. We should keep seeking Him until the door is opened. God desires our salvation.

Next our persistence should overflow into our witnessing. Charles Spurgeon said, "If sinners be damned, at least let them leap to Hell over our dead bodies. And if they perish, let them perish with our arms wrapped about their knees, imploring them to stay. If Hell must be filled, let it be filled in the teeth of our exertions, and let not one go unwarned and unprayed for." We need to be passionate about the lost. We need to make sure they know and accept the truth.

Persistence should then move into our everyday life. Calvin Coolidge said, "Nothing in this world can take the place of persistence. Talent will not: nothing is more common than unsuccessful men with talent. Genius will not; unrewarded genius is almost a proverb. Education will not: the world is full of educated derelicts. Persistence and determination alone are omnipotent." Hard work wins. As a coach, I always liked players who refused to lose over talent. Talent tends to get lazy.

People who stop should not say that it cannot be done. They do not know.

You probably do not know Frank Reich. Frank was a quarterback who did not throw in the towel. While in college at Maryland, his team was losing to Miami 31-0. He orchestrated an incredible comeback for the victory. He was picked up by the Buffalo Bills. In a playoff game, they were losing to the Houston Oilers 35-3, yet again came back to win. He did not quit. As the expression goes, "He was a winner, not a whiner."

Paul summarized it well in Philippians 3:14, ***"I press on toward the goal for the prize of the upward call of God in Christ Jesus."*** I do not know what God's plan is for you, but press on.

1 + 0 = 0: DEVOTION 5

FAVORITE TEACHER

Dr. Randy T. Johnson | Growth Pastor

While being a pastor, I was a school teacher for 29 years. I taught middle school, high school, and even at a college for five years. I thoroughly enjoyed it. All the age groups brought their own challenges, but blessings. However, it was not my goal to be a life-long teacher. My goal is to be a life-long learner. Even while teaching, I often was learning. I "lead" three growth communities, but I am always the student. I want to be teachable.

The only true life-long teacher is Jesus. John chapter 20 contains the resurrection of Jesus Christ. Mary Magdalene notices the stone had been moved away from the tomb of Jesus. She went and told Peter and John, who came running back. His body was gone. Mary stood off to the side of the tomb weeping. Jesus approached her. She did not pay much attention as she thought it was the gardener. They had a brief discussion. Verse 16 says, *"Jesus said to her, 'Mary.' She turned and said to him in Aramaic, 'Rabboni!' (which means Teacher)."* I appreciate that the actual text tells us that she calls Him Teacher. She uses the word for rabbi, which we understand means teacher. Of all the words she could have used, she chooses "Teacher." He is so much more, but "Teacher" is the title that she felt brought Him the most honor.

Jesus knew He was to be a teacher. John 14:6-7 says, *"Jesus said to him, 'I am the way, and the truth, and the life. No one comes to the Father except through me."* Only a confident teacher says that he knows the way. He is the guide, the leader. He has the truth. He knows how we are to live. He embraces the privilege and responsibility of being an instructor. He has information they need. It is bursting out of Him. He is living His life for them. He wakes up thinking about His students.

Do you have a favorite teacher from your childhood? What was it that you liked about them? Did they believe in you and push you to a level you did not think you could go? Did you always know they cared about you? That is the teacher Jesus is. In Matthew 8:19 we read, ***"And a scribe came up and said to him, 'Teacher, I will follow you wherever you go.'"*** We probably all have had a teacher we wished we could have for more than one year. Jesus is the teacher who cares about you; He even loves you. He believes in you and can take you to levels you never imagined. He is the Master Teacher.

The Teacher above all teachers wrote a book. What have you learned today?

1 + 0 = 0: DEVOTION 6

3 THINGS

Dr. Randy T. Johnson | Growth Pastor

I started regularly saying three things to my children since they were toddlers, "I love you, you are the best, because God made you special." I have always wanted them to know I love them and God loves them. I also want them to know that God is "El." He is The Strong One. He created them and they are "fearfully and wonderfully made." He is stronger than any other choice. He will overcome all obstacles. We can depend on God.

I want them to know that this Strong One has a plan for them. Jeremiah 29:11 says, *"For I know the plans I have for you, declares the LORD, plans for welfare and not for evil, to give you a future and a hope."* I want them to seek out His plan. I want them to be blessed.

God is the Strong One. No other god can even come close. Exodus 15:2 says, *"The LORD is my strength and my song, and he has become my salvation; this is my God, and I will praise him, my father's God, and I will exalt him."* He is my strength and salvation. I strive to praise and exalt Him with my words and actions. He is God.

Deuteronomy 7:9 says, *"Know therefore that the LORD your God is God, the faithful God who keeps covenant and steadfast love with those who love him and keep his commandments, to a thousand generations."* He is God. Love and faithfulness flow from Him. He looks for this in us, too.

"El" is such a common name for Him. It is used more than 200 times in the Old Testament. We often call Him by this name without even realizing it. Isra-el (wrestles with God), Beth-el

(House of God), and El-isha (God is salvation) are a few examples. Even Superman's original name was Kal-El (swift god).

"El" wants a relationship with us. The only way to Him is through His Son Jesus. John 14:6 says, ***"Jesus said to him, 'I am the way, and the truth, and the life. No one comes to the Father except through me.'"*** Jesus is "the" way to the Father. There is no other.

As I close out this book on parables and a study on the names of Jesus and God, I want to leave you with a few thoughts. First, God loves you. John 3:16 says, ***"For God so loved the world, that he gave his only Son, that whoever believes in him should not perish but have eternal life."*** Second, you are the best. So, be the best you can. Step out of your comfort zone and follow Christ to the next level. Third, God made you special. God never says, "Oops." He created you just the way He wanted.

Finally, one of my favorite verses is 3 John 1:4, ***"I have no greater joy than to hear that my children are walking in the truth."*** Walk in the truth.

16

REACH, GATHER, GROW, AND BACK TO REACH

Dr. Randy T. Johnson | Growth Pastor

Matthew 28:19-20 is referred to as the Great Commission. It is the last two verses of the book of Matthew. Jesus has already risen from the dead, and He gets the disciples together for some final words. It is a coach's last pep talk as the players enter the arena for a big game. He says, ***"Go therefore and make disciples of all nations, baptizing them in the name of the Father and of the Son and of the Holy Spirit, teaching them to observe all that I have commanded you. And behold, I am with you always, to the end of the age."***

It is these verses that are the basis for who we are as the Church: The Church exists to glorify God by reaching the world, gathering with the saints, and growing in the Word.

This mission seems quite clear from Jesus' words:

"Go therefore and make disciples of all nations," (glorify God by reaching the world)

"baptizing them in the name of the Father and of the Son and of the Holy Spirit," (glorify God by gathering with the saints)

"teaching them to observe all that I have commanded you. And behold, I am with you always, to the end of the age" (glorify God by growing in the Word).

This process is not a straight line with an ending point. It is more like a spiral as we reach, gather, grow we should then want to be reaching more of the world, gathering, growing, and so on.

Please remember the focus of every step – Glorify God!

Reaching the World – Reach

"Go therefore and make disciples of all nations," (glorify God by reaching the world).

"Every Christian is either a missionary or an imposter." Charles Spurgeon

What does this quote mean? _____
_____
_____

Do you agree or disagree with the quote? Why? _____
_____
_____
_____

Acts 1:8
"But you will receive power when the Holy Spirit has come upon you, and you will be my witnesses in Jerusalem and in all Judea and Samaria, and to the end of the earth."

Is anything implied by these geographical locations? _____

_____
_____
_____

How would you phrase these locations in "your world" today?

_____
_____
_____

How can people be reached today that did not exist 2,000 (or even 20) years ago? _____

_____
_____

Are we creative and intentional in reaching others? _____

_____
_____
_____

What resources do we have that we are not using well in reaching others? _____

_____
_____

How and when can we use them? _____

_____
_____

Matthew 5:16
"In the same way, let your light shine before others, so that they may see your good works and give glory to your Father who is in heaven."

What does *"let your light shine"* mean? _____
_____
_____
_____

Mark 16:15-16
"And he said to them, 'Go into all the world and proclaim the gospel to the whole creation. Whoever believes and is baptized will be saved, but whoever does not believe will be condemned.'"

What does the word ***"proclaim"*** mean? _____
_____
_____
_____

Does this allow for the belief that everyone will go to Heaven?
_____
_____
_____

"God save us from living in comfort while sinners are sinking into hell!" Charles Spurgeon

What "comforts" are distracting us from reaching us with the Gospel? _____
_____
_____
_____
_____

TESTIMONY 1

CHUCK LINDSEY
Reach Pastor

New Year's Eve, 1980, near midnight, the phone rings and my mother is told that my father and his friend were in a fatal car accident. They had both been drinking that night and were on their way back from getting more beer when they hit the flatbed of a turning diesel truck. Danny died instantly, my father suffered major internal injury and took his last breath three days later. I was just three years old, my sister was 1, and my mother was 19.

That night began a series of events that ultimately led to my rescue from sin, death, and hell by the One who loved me and gave Himself for me.

Four years passed and my mother was (I now believe) divinely introduced to my dad. They were married a year later, and though none of us yet knew Him, the work of Jesus to rescue us all was at work.

Tuesday morning, March 14th, 4:15 am, the phone rings again... my dad has been in a near fatal car accident and is being taken by ambulance to the ER. He survived. He was on his way to work that morning, and it was very early... like 3 am early. As he sped down the unlit street, he suddenly saw the reflectors of the flatbed of a diesel truck that was turning around. With less than a second to stop, he realized he was going to hit it and says that at that moment he felt someone push him down and hold him there as the car went under the truck's bed. The entire top of the car was peeled back. He was in the hospital for three days. But he survived.

Two weeks later, Easter Sunday morning, March 26, 1989, 9:30 am, my parents, sister, and I get out of our car in the church parking lot for Easter service. My grandmother, who had invited us, saved us all a seat. What felt like hours of preaching (to a kid), was only a few minutes and at the end of the sermon my parents stood up and began to walk down the stairs. I thought we were leaving. We were not. We were doing the craziest thing I had ever seen... we were walking forward to the front of the stage. My parents were repenting of their sin and receiving Jesus.

Our lives were immediately different from that moment forward. We were "church people." By that I mean, we were at church, a lot. Sundays, Wednesday nights, Youth groups, camps, bake sales, men's groups and women's studies and, and, and... Somehow, in all of this, I managed not to be saved at all. Somehow in all of this, I managed not to see my need to be saved, not see my need for Jesus. Somehow, I was able to go to church and completely ignore everything except my friends, and whatever cute girl was there.

It was January 1996, 6:15 am, in the back bedroom of my grandmother's home in Riverside California. I was sixteen years old. I was running from, what I now realize, was myself. My world was falling apart. To be more accurate, I was falling apart. My sin was heavy, pushing down on me and had become a load I could no longer carry. I was angry. I was consumed with myself. I was lost. Sitting there, at my drawing table, with the shattered remains of a mechanical pencil I had just driven into the table top in anger... I looked over and saw the Bible my parents bought me sticking out of my duffle bag. The thought came, "Well, I call myself a Christian and I never read that thing. What have I got to lose, maybe it will help." Three chapters into the book of Matthew and I was flat on the floor, face down, weeping in repentance to Jesus. Suddenly, this "faker" had become a "follower." I read and read and read and read the Scriptures... night and day, day and night. I like to say that I was born again by the Word of God. I would read for hours, stop to eat, then hurry back to read, fall asleep, wake, and read. For the first time, I heard the voice of Jesus, understanding His Word, hearing His leading and teaching... feeling His presence. I did not want it to end. I was afraid that it was eventually going to "go away" and so I read and read. I read through the entire New Testament in a week and then began on the Old Testament.

It was September 1996 in Murrieta, California. I entered Bible college. Two years later I graduated with a degree in theology and pastoral ministry. During college, I served as the youth pastor at a local church. Out of college, I was called to continue as a youth pastor in my home church in Michigan. Seven years later, the Lord called me to start a church in the city of Flint. I pastored that church for six years until the Lord called us to Riverside, California where I was an assistant pastor, get this... at the church, my parents walked forward at to receive Christ all those years before! Harvest Christian Fellowship. The Lord is amazing, isn't He?

I have been a radically different person since that day in 1996. Jesus rescued me that day. He loved me and brought me to Himself with the truth of His Word. As I write this, with tears in my eyes, it is a joy to say that it was 20 years ago... He is the love of my heart, and His will is the burning desire of my life. All praise to the One who "loved us and gave Himself for us!"

TESTIMONY 2

ORALIA LINDSEY
Wife of Pastor Chuck Lindsey

My childhood is full of so many ups and downs like most of you. Sadly, my biological father had a major drug and pornography problem. Our childhood was full of unpredictability because of it. My mom struggled to provide for us because we could not depend on my father. I was molested in elementary school by a close family friend, and that was a heavy burden I did not know how to handle. My parents made sure we never saw that man again, but the weight was on my shoulders for years to come.

My mom raised us as Jehovah Witness because she lost her third child to SIDS, (Nina was only two months old) and was looking for an answer to why God would allow her baby to die and they gave her a comforting enough answer. My parents divorced by the time we were in middle school and not too long after our stepdad came into the picture. Boy did we hate him. We did not have many rules before him and to be honest we kind of walked all over my mom. She worked a lot to provide for us and did not have the energy to fight with us. As time went on, we came to realize what a gift our stepdad was. He is a man that decided to love my mom and her three unruly kids. We love him dearly and thank the Lord for him.

A missionary family came back to the states and decided that their neighborhood was their new mission field. They began reaching out to all the kids and teaching us about Jesus Christ. My mom reluctantly allowed us to go. As I learned, I thought I was growing, but I did not realize that all that information was just going into my brain and not changing who I was. At 14 years old I had the opportunity to attend a math program at a college. It was my first taste of (almost) complete freedom. I met new friends and even told girls about Christianity. By the end of the program, I had begun to spend time with a girl that was smoking pot. A couple of nights before the program was done I had the opportunity to smoke pot with her...and I took it. Friends that I had made were so upset that they left and told our counselors. At 1:00 am my mom had to drive an hour to get me. She would not even speak to me. My stepdad was so disappointed that I would even consider doing drugs after knowing how it affected our lives from my biological father. That night I realized that if I did not surrender my life to Jesus, I would completely destroy my life. Everything changed that night. I wanted to please Jesus with my life. The Lord's plan for my life was SO much better than ANYTHING I could have ever dreamed. I am married to my best friend, we have four amazing kids, and we get to serve Jesus and his people.

TESTIMONY 3

JOSH COMBS
Lead Pastor

I am a church rat. A PK (Pastor's kid for those who do not know the lingo). My Dad became a Youth and Children's Pastor at a small Fundamental Baptist church about 45 minutes north of Detroit when I was one month old. From there my love affair with what I thought was the church began. I was at "church" Sunday morning, Sunday night, Wednesday night, special events, and visitation (or soul winning) night. My car seat was put in the front seat of the bus because my mom picked up kids and teens in the inner city of Pontiac. She took me along. As I grew, I was part of Sunday school, AWANA (yup, I have the trophies, patches, and books to prove it), camp groups, mission trips, youth group, Christmas productions, Easter productions, and blah...blah... blah. I am sure you get the point, even to boredom. I know, I am feeling sick to my stomach just typing this list. I preached my first sermon in first grade to my Christian school and had a few more sermons under my belt before elementary school ended. I started singing towards the end of junior high, so preaching was replaced with "special music." I was the quintessential church kid. I knew more Scripture than most adults. I did not need a hymn book because I knew most of those too. Now you might be thinking, "Ugh...what a miserable life!" But the truth is, I loved every moment! The "church" was my favorite place to be and the center of my life. I loved the smell of the old building. I loved the events. I loved the potlucks. I loved the whole place. It was my home. I remember the summer between 8th and 9th grade being so concerned that with high school career starting I would not be able to be heavily involved in the "church" building project. This was a major concern in my young life. During high school, I lead Bible studies at my house and my public high school. I coordinated major youth and even church-wide events. I wrote curriculum for elementary camps. I even attended a private Christian school located in a "church" from the time I was three until the end of junior high. I graduated from a Christian college and went to seminary. My life was a beautiful spectacle of churchy-ness. And somewhere in this mess, I got saved.

I do not remember the sermon or even who preached, but in my mind, I can transport myself back to that exact moment. I was standing in the front row with my dad at the close of a Wednesday night revival service. I looked up at my dad, as a just a young boy, and said, "Dad, I need to be saved." That night, in hindsight, was the true epitome of childlike faith. I knew I was destined to Hell because of my sin, and only Jesus could save me. I was baptized on a Sunday night a few weeks later.

I do not have an exciting or riveting testimony by most standards. I was not addicted to drugs or divorced five times or a professional athlete. My life was not at rock-bottom. I was five years old. But something happened over the next few decades that I am afraid will take the rest of my life to fix. As I meet people now in my role as a Pastor, I am amazed that regardless of the denominational background, so many of us have similar stories. Maybe you do not have the depth of church cred, but you have accumulated incredible amounts of religious baggage that Jesus never intended for you to have. Because of my story of God's incredible grace, my heart burns with a passion for the religious. For you. The 'churchy' people. The holy rollers. The Jesus freaks. The Pharisees. I was not rescued out of an abusive family. My parents are incredible people. I was not rescued out of alcoholism or drug addiction. I was rescued out of religion. I was rescued out of "church."

The Apostle Paul writes in Philippians 3:
"If anyone else thinks he has reason for confidence in the

flesh, I have more: circumcised on the eighth day, of the people of Israel, of the tribe of Benjamin, a Hebrew of Hebrews; as to the law, a Pharisee; as to zeal, a persecutor of the church; as to righteousness under the law, blameless. But whatever gain I had, I counted as loss for the sake of Christ. Indeed, I count everything as loss because of the surpassing worth of knowing Christ Jesus my Lord."

This is Paul's story. He had all of the religious credentials but was empty and hopeless. Then he met Jesus. And that encounter on the road to Damascus changed everything. This is my story. I had all the church credentials but found much of it to be "dung" (Philippians 3:7, KJV). I am not Paul and am hesitant to even draw this comparison. But I do recognize, that without the Gospel of Jesus Christ, religious credentials mean "jack- squat" (Quoting my favorite motivational speaker). So, here is my mess, my story, which I have heard echoed thousands of times in coffee shops, counseling appointments, and countless other places. I am hoping that Jesus can save you too from "church."

TESTIMONY 4

KEN PERRY

Assistant to the Reach Pastor

Time sure flies when you are having fun. With that said, I cannot believe it has been 32 years since I made a decision to accept Jesus Christ as my Lord and Savior. Sometimes I think I should be further along in my faith, but there is a great assurance in the fact that I know I am right where God wants me to be.

Testimony is defined for us this way, "A public recounting of a religious conversion or experience." That is it, nothing flashy or earth shattering. Just our retelling of the single most important moment in our Christian lives. For some, this conversion comes as a realization that the particular path they were headed down was going to be a dead end, that the choices being made were not turning out the way they had planned. We know this experience as a "Rock Bottom" conversion. The reality of the situation so confronts a person that they understand they cannot do life under their power anymore. There is a desire for spiritual intervention, and the only way to do that is to allow God to have total control of their lives. As the title suggests; however, that was not me.

I grew up in a loving middle-class home. That is not to say we did not have our fair share of issues, but I did have everything I needed and most things I wanted. My dad coached many of my sports teams and for most of my adolescence, my mom stayed at home to raise my brother and me. I began wrestling in high school and started dating the stats girl (probably in the hopes that my scores would improve). Before long, she asked if I would like to go to a youth group event at her church. I had gone to church as a kid… well, a truer version would be that I was put in the back of the station wagon and made to go to church with my mom and her friend. I had no other experience with the church up until I was asked to youth group at 15. I said yes because I wanted to be with her but did not realize the impact it would have on me.

Two things happened that night. First, I saw that the Youth Pastor was my wrestling coach. You might say no big deal, but it showed me you could combine the worlds of athletics and religion which was a new concept that helped as I started processing Christianity. I did not have to give up what I loved to do to come to Christ. The second thing was that I felt an amazing energy created by this group. I had felt the energy coming from crowds before (there is nothing like wrestling in front of a packed gymnasium) and it truly can be electric. This was different, though. I saw every type of person from my high school in that room. Silly teenagers that we were, we had to keep up our personas on campus, but at this youth group, I saw barriers broken down and kids having a great time worshipping Jesus together. I can not help but think of the book of Esther when I think back to this group... **"for such a time as this."**

That group became my life. Sure, I still played sports, but the group of friends that came from this time was so much more important. They had the effect of cementing my heart to Christ before I even became a believer. After about a year of listening to the messages I came to the biggest realization of my life, and this is what I want you to grasp dear brothers and sisters. No matter where you come from, what you did, rock bottom or not, we are all separated from God by sin (Isaiah 59:2) until we ask Him for forgiveness and accept Him as our Lord and Savior. I was no better than the drug dealer, thief, adulterer, or murderer. The degree of sin was different according to the world, but God does not grade on a curve. He only sees the heart and mine was just as wicked according to Jeremiah 17:9, **"The heart is deceitful**

above all things, and desperately sick; who can understand it?" Unless I made a decision to follow Him, I was eternally lost.

So, that is what I did at the ripe age of sixteen, I settled the separation issue once and for all, and as you can imagine, it was the best decision of my life. Not everything has been rosy and right, but let me encourage you with this, it is not supposed to be. John 16:33 clearly tells us, ***"in this world you WILL have tribulation (trouble). But take heart; I have overcome the world."***

When the world knocks us down, like the big bully that it is, we have an advocate that is bigger than anything the world can throw at us. If you are on the fence about this thing called Christianity, settle the separation issue today. If you have strayed from God like many of us have, take a note from the prodigal story and realize you are better off being a "hired hand" in the Kingdom rather than a "king" in the world. Come back to Christ while there is still time. Personal experience tells me you will not be sorry you did.

TESTIMONY 5

MARK O'CONNOR
Student Director

I always thought my story was pretty lame. I did not have this rock-bottom-I-found-Jesus moment. I was not a bad guy. I grew up in a home where we went to church every week. I was baptized as an infant. I received my first communion and was even confirmed when I was a teenager. I received these sacraments, and they were supposed to be done in the church in which I was raised. Youth group was fun in the summer when we played softball, but I always wondered why we did not learn more about God in those times. I was along for the ride. When my dad stopped waking me up every Sunday morning, I stopped going to mass. I just kind of lived my life from there. I still was not a bad guy. I was the guy my friends turned to when they needed to talk. There was no drinking or drugs. No smoking. I may have been at the party, but I was the one making sure everybody was ok.

I was not perfect. I messed up; made a bunch of mistakes and got into some trouble. But I was a teenager after all. Life was good. You could say I was kind of cruising thru life. Work was good. Somewhere around my 19th birthday, I met the woman who would later become my wife. Jamie and I developed a great friendship that blossomed into a great relationship. She had recently had a daughter when we started dating. The first time my parents met her, we were walking into the same entrance at the mall and Haley was with us. This was a mildly awkward moment.

We were engaged to be married after a year and a half. During the planning of our wedding, we discovered that Jamie was going to give birth to our first son. My world was now upside down. Here I was, 20 years old. I was about to be the head of a family. To say I was overwhelmed was an understatement. How was I going to handle this? What was I going to do?

I went on a weekend trip to a business conference in North Carolina. I do not remember most of the speakers that were there or what they said. Then came a church service on Sunday morning. A speaker by the name of Josh McDowell came to the stage. He spoke about fatherhood. He spoke about the responsibility I had as a father to raise my children and how important it is to make God a part of that. It was my "light bulb" moment. I do not remember the preacher from that service, but I know I gave my life to Jesus that morning.

We drove home, and I remember the preacher saying I needed to find a good, Bible preaching church. My brother in law pointed me to the River in Waterford (at that time, known as Faith). We were immediately drawn to Pastor Jim's preaching style and connected quickly. In May of 2001, we were married in this church. A desire for God's Word burned inside me, as it usually does for new Christians. After a while, that began to fade a bit, and I fell back into the normal routine.

Jamie began serving a lot in the church, but I was not there yet. After a time, I went to a snow camp with Pastor Jayson and the teens. A small fire began to burn again. It grew as I began to serve more and get into studying the Bible again. I was working retail at the time, and it was difficult to get a set schedule to serve consistently, but I did when I could.

In 2012, we made a huge change and went to serve in a small church in Walled Lake. It was the area where I went to high school, and to be honest, God called us there when Pastor Jim first started preaching there. At the time, I thought I knew what was better for me than God did. So I naturally fought it. Then Pastor Chris Doak asked us to serve with him to work with the student ministry. So we made our way to First Baptist Church of Walled Lake, now known as Market Street Church. My eyes were opened to the incredible work God does in our lives when we completely commit to his will. Somebody asked me one night as we were leaving youth group if I had ever considered being a pastor. I would love to say that in that instant I said yes, but I laughed. Then, as He so often does, God decided otherwise. As I continued to serve faithfully, my mindset shifted to a place where I longed to serve God more, and I made the decision the follow that course for my life.

So I started school to begin that process. I worked full-time, served pretty close to full-time, and took classes to obtain a degree in Pastoral Ministry. Eventually, I was hired on a part-time basis at Market Street and became so entrenched in the workings of the church. I learned so much in this time and am forever grateful for my time spent and friends made in Walled Lake. But once again, God stirred up our lives. And here I am, back home where my journey started. I am blessed to be serving the Lord full-time at this big white church on Airport Road. My office is two doors down from the office where Pastor Jim counseled Jamie and me before our wedding. It is the same office where Pastor Chris asked us if we would pray about joining him in Walled Lake. I cannot wait to see what God has in store for our family and me.

TESTIMONY 6

JOHN CARTER
Director of Finance & HR

I have lots of favorite passages in the Bible, but the one that I think without a doubt I can always fall back on is Hebrews 11:1. This is the passage that challenged my life, and it forced me to dig into the reality of who Jesus Christ is.

"Faith is the <u>substance</u> of things hoped for, the <u>evidence</u> of things not seen."

It is a simple passage with a lot of deep implications to consider. The two underlined words, to me, are the most significant aspects of this passage. What are the things we hope for, but cannot see? How do we determine the substance of that hope and by what evidence are we challenging our faith? It was through the deep thinking and processing of this passage that I asked myself, *"What substance did I have, that would give me hope?"*

That is not an easy question to answer right off the cuff? I mean there were several things I had tried to fill in the blank spot called substance for hope. You can fill in the blank! *"My faith is based on _____ (fill in the blank), This is what my hope in life is based on!"*

The "blank" can be anything: money, job/career, family, friends, self, good deeds, church, religion, girlfriend/boyfriend, a prayer, baptism, church attendance. It can go on and on with things we put in place of Jesus Christ. I was a missionary kid in Japan for nearly 17 years. I grew up in the church and was very much a part of the religious entity call "the church." I knew the rules, knew what to say, and how to act, had the list of "do" and "do not" down. I failed to find any substance in those things. One of the cool things about the book of Hebrews is that there is only one correct answer. You cannot have multiple right answers; you only get one! Take some time and reflect on what is the substance of your faith, is it Jesus Christ? There is nothing that will sustain your hope for the long run other than Jesus.

The second part of the passage talks about evidence. This evidence for me was a big deal! You might ask, Why? Well, when I was dealing with this passage, I was atheistic in my worldview, that means I openly claimed there was no God. I had abandoned the religion I had grown up with and decided that the opposite of religion must have more substance and evidence for a life of hope. I had a hard time believing in something that I could not see. Maybe, just maybe, you can relate to this struggle? It was not uncommon for me to speak of religion as a crutch, or a device created by the weak to deal with the harsh realities of life. I struggled with the aspect of there being evidence! I was able to understand that if there was evidence, and if there is substance to this "idea" called faith, then that would mean I could touch and feel it. It would be tangible. It forced me to look at what my faith, or lack of faith, had produced. I had to go through and analyze what substance I had that gave me hope. The lifestyle I had chosen had led to very little by which I could say I was hopeful. The devil has a way of enticing us with the short term; it only distracts us from dealing with the truth. In the short term, money, partying, women, all seemed sufficient to keep me full of hope. Then it was not enough! The party always came to an end, money never quite seemed to last, and the high never lasted. You always came down, and the lows were low, and the hangover almost always came the next day. We as humans have this innate ability to mask and numb our hopelessness with short-term fixes that do not fix anything.

When I share my story of how a came to know Jesus, I will, without hesitation, quote this passage. It does not matter which side of the proverbial aisle you come from, religious or irreligious, this passage can be a great passage to get you thinking. For me, I feel like I tried both ways. I lived for the longest time having prayed a prayer thinking that is all there was to it. I had my "fire insurance" so to speak, but no real evidence that I knew Christ personally. Church attendance, offerings, a magic prayer, and good deeds do not save you. I also tried the "do as I please" and disregarded the existence of God. Sin is a real thing, Hell is a real place, and God does exist. Just because we cannot see Him does not make Him anymore fake than the wind. Either lifestyle, religious or irreligious, leads to the same hopeless emptiness. There is only one way to have a hope that is both substantial and has the evidence of outlasting anything else, in fact, it is an eternal hope. If Jesus Christ is not the substance of your faith, let me encourage you to examine your faith, examine the evidence for Jesus Christ, and examine the substance in the Scripture for who He is.

17

GATHERING WITH THE SAINTS

"***B**aptizing them in the name of the Father and of the Son and of the Holy Spirit,*" (glorify God by gathering with the saints).

"Church attendance is as vital to a disciple as a transfusion of rich, healthy blood to a sick man." Dwight L. Moody

How is church attendance vital? _____
_____
_____

How can we improve our gatherings so that it is more vital?
_____
_____
_____

Hebrews 10:24-25
"And let us consider how to stir up one another to love and good works, not neglecting to meet together, as is the habit of some, but encouraging one another, and all the more as you see the Day drawing near."

In what ways can we encourage someone else? _____
_____
_____
_____

Do you have an example how you were encouraged? _____
_____
_____
_____

Acts 2:42-47

"And they devoted themselves to the apostles' teaching and the fellowship, to the breaking of bread and the prayers. And awe came upon every soul, and many wonders and signs were being done through the apostles. And all who believed were together and had all things in common. And they were selling their possessions and belongings and distributing the proceeds to all, as any had need. And day by day, attending the temple together and breaking bread in their homes, they received their food with glad and generous hearts, praising God and having favor with all the people. And the Lord added to their number day by day those who were being saved."

List the different things they did when they came together.
_____
_____
_____

Is our Church consistent with this description of the early church?
_____
_____
_____

What items do you like about our Gatherings? _____
_____
_____
_____

"Though true Christianity uniquely involves a personal relationship with Jesus Christ, it is also a corporate experience... Christians cannot grow spiritually as they ought to in isolation from one another." Pastor Gene Getz

Do you agree or disagree with this quote? Why? _____
_____
_____
_____

"An empty tomb proves Christianity; an empty church denies it." Author unknown

Do you agree or disagree with this quote? Why? _____
_____
_____
_____

What should we pray on our way to a gathering? _____
_____
_____
_____

TESTIMONY 7

CALEB COMBS
Gathering Pastor

When thinking about my story and road with Jesus Christ, I can simply describe it as "NOT DESERVED!" So many times God has intervened and directed my paths, and man was I way off track. Proverbs 3:5-6 tells us to trust in the Lord with all of your heart and lean not on your own understandings and in all your ways He will direct your paths. I have truly found these truths to be evident in my life. I have been blessed with an incredible family. My Dad and Mom are superheroes in the faith. I do not just say that to compliment them, but I truly believe it. Knowing what my parents came from and how they got to the point of being used by God to do incredible things, I just stand back in awe of how incredible God is. They both have a passion for God and His people and would fight all of Hell to try and reach just one more per son. They raised my brothers, sister, and me in the church. I am sure you have heard the adage, "Every time the church doors were open we were there." That was us as a family. Sunday mornings, Sunday nights, Wednesday nights and usually a couple of other days sprinkled in throughout the week.

It is crazy to think of the incredible things I have been able to see God do. In my own life, the salvation story is much different. I heard many stories of crack addicts coming to Jesus and stopping their addictions only by the power of Jesus. There are miraculous stories of God just stepping into someone's life and making them new. I can remember thinking to myself, man I wish I had one of "those" stories. It was 1990, and I was 5 1/2 years old. I had to say half because at that age you included halves because if not you lied and just said 6 to round up! At that time, we had a dynamic kids' ministry (thankful for a church that continues to find children important and puts effort into kids' ministry). As the kids' service was ending, they gave an altar call and asked if anyone wanted to receive Jesus into their heart? I felt the Holy Spirit speaking into my life and a conviction I could not deny. Yes, at just five years old, I felt conviction. The only problem for me is that I was extremely conscious of what people thought of me. We will talk more of this as well go, but it is something I have fought my entire life. SO... I fought off what others thought and raised my hand. A man named Doug Brady came by and took me to the last room on the right, at the end of the hallway and led me to the Lord. To this day, I am blessed to have Doug as a friend. He led me through the sinner's prayer, and I knew that I needed Jesus to forgive me of my sins. That night I was baptize d at Sunday night church by my dad.

On that Spring day, my walk with Jesus began. I can remember lots of details and faces, so make sure you talk to your children about salvation and their need for Jesus. I know with my kids it is easy just to think they are kids and they will figure it out. I am thankful for men and women who constantly helped me see Jesus. Now the Proverbs 3 verses came into effect in my life. Man did I try to walk on my path and lean on my understanding. I constantly worried about what others thought, so I was led astray by things. Far from perfect and being convicted of my sins as a teenager God was constantly working on my behalf. I tended to have a bit of a mouth (ok still working on that), and many times I would have to go to God in repentance of things I said or did. As a teenager, while my u ncle Steve was preaching I felt called into ministry, but this something that scared the living daylights out of me! First, my parents were superheroes, and I could never live up to them. Secondly, what would people think? These two huge obstacles were difficult for me to overcome. The enemy constantly threw these things in my face and took me as far away from ministry as I could get.

In high school, I was a pretty good basketball player and had a few colleges looking at me to play at their school. In my senior year, I got an offer to play at a little small Bible college in Grand Rapids, named Grace Bible College. Not knowing God was leading and directing my paths to this "Bible" college, all I wanted to do was play basketball and meet girls. So I committed to going to this college, and in the fall of 2002, I headed off to Grand Rapids, MI. Man, did I make lots of mistakes, but somehow God continued to lead and guide me. Grace (as in God's unnerved favor) is something I look back and stand amazed at how God showed me favor. I am not sure if it was the many people who tell me that they prayed for me constantly or God just feeling sorry for me, but He continued to bless and lead me. I met this amazing, smoking hot girl when I was a sophomore in college and man did she get lucky (just kidding)! We started dating and ended up getting married between my junior and senior years of college. There are lots of stories where I messed that relationship up and should have lost her as well, yet God constantly worked in my life. I am so thankful for her and helping me become the man I am today.

I guess what I am trying to tell you is that I have been blessed WAY beyond what I deserve. That is my life and my salvation story. I deserved death and separation from God forever. Just as I should not have anything I have in my life, however, God is incredible and saved me! I could sit here and tell you of many more mistakes and many times I ran from God i n what I call my "Jonah Journeys," but each time I ran, God came and got me by putting people in my life that helped steer and direct me, (thank you Kevin Dean, Gabe Marshall, Bob Marshall, Steve and Stacey Shadley, and many others I could spend naming and taking up this whole thing). In summary, Lamentations 3 shows my heart and is something I cling to every day; ***"Yet I still dare to hope*** *when I remember this: **The faithful love of the Lord never ends! His mercies never cease. Great is his faithfulness; his mercies begin afresh each morning. I say to myself, 'The Lord is my inheritance; therefore, I will hope in him!'"*** I am a walking example of God's grace and mercy being new every day; man do I need them! I am thankful for the men and women God has placed in my life. From parents and grandparents committed to the work of Jesus Christ, to the people who put up with a dumb kid in his late teens and early twenties; God directed my path and has led me to a place of thankfulness!

TESTIMONY 8

SIERRA COMBS
Women's Ministry Director

A ugust 23, 1963, Southern California. It was my grandma's 29th birthday. Her husband, an unsaved professional golfer, told her he would take her anywhere she wanted to go for her birthday. She just had to pick the place, and they would hop in the car and go. My grandpa was always a spoiler. I remember when I was growing up how he would take us on the most extravagant outings. We would shop all day, go to high tea at the Ritz, and he just loved to take us to the best steakhouses in town. Everything with him was so special, and he just loved to spoil the people that he loved. So my gram could have picked anywhere to go and anything to do, no questions asked. Now, my grandma has always been an avid prayer warrior - one of those amazing crazy people who wakes up at 4:30 in the morning to spend time in the Word and on her knees deep in prayer for every single person she loves (I am not a morning person and keep waiting for this gene to kick in, but so far no luck).

She wanted nothing more for her husband than for him to accept that same wonderful gift of salvation that she had been given years past. So on her 29th birthday, she asked him to take her to the LA Coliseum to hear Billy Graham preach. Personally, I would have picked Disneyland, but I am not nearly as insightful as she is. Besides wanting to go and hear a good word from the famous preacher, she felt a tugging from the Holy Spirit to take my grandpa there that day. Long story short, God moved in his heart, he accepted Christ as His Savior from those Coliseum seats, retired from his golfing career, sold his golf course, moved his family across the country, and dove headfirst into full-time ministry at a tiny little Bible College in Grand Rapids, MI. It is the same tiny college my mom attended and met my dad, a basketball player from Ohio who loved Jesus. It is the same tiny college I attended and met my husband, a basketball player from Michigan who loves Jesus. I have always been so thankful to my grandma for taking my grandpa to that crusade. She always says it was the best birthday gift she could have ever been given - God's grace given to the man she loved the most. What a beautiful testimony! What a beautiful legacy. A legacy that led to me.

Sometimes I wish I had a testimony like that. One of those amazing "come to Jesus" moments that moves people to tears and points to the amazing saving grace of the Savior. But that is not my story. I do remember sitting on my bed when I was 4, asking Jesus "into my heart," but that is it. There was no night and day change in my little life, as far as I know. I do not remember a time when I did not love Jesus. There has never been a time that I was not in church several times a week, learning about Him, and worshiping Him. Summers were spent at church camp and VBS. Family meals were spent around the dinner table playing Bible trivia or talking about the things God was doing in our hearts. I knew no other life than the life of a super involved church kid. Because I did not have that "light bulb" moment and rapid heart change that so many people experience after they accept Christ at an older age, sometimes I would feel less legitimate than others or even question if I was truly saved. When it was testimony sharing time in youth group, I would sink in my chair or excuse myself to the bathroom because I felt like I had nothing extraordinary to say. But over the years, God has shown me that even though I did not experience a Saul to Paul-like conversion, I still have a story. There is no dull salvation. God loved me so much that He became flesh to die on a cross and pay the penalty for my sin. He saved me, changed my heart, and WILL continue to change my heart until my time on this earth is done. I am not who I was when I was 4, or 17, or even last year. Praise God for that! I yearn to be more like Jesus with each passing day, and while I fail so often, I still press towards that mark. Even though my story may not be the most exciting, I have 27 years of God's grace over my life - grace that I need every single day.

My family said our final earthly goodbye to my grandpa on August 23, 2008 - my grandma's 74th birthday and his 45th spiritual birthday. Instead of a funeral, we had a birthday party, and we celebrated the life of a godly man, his faithful wife, and most importantly the God who saved them both. My grams always says that no one could ever top that birthday gift God gave her back in 1963 - His grace given to the man she loved the most. I am so thankful for that legacy, and I pray it will be passed on to my children and their children and beyond. And someday when my kids are asked to share their story, I hope that it turns out to be as amazing as mine.

TESTIMONY 9

TREVOR COLE

Nearly from the moment I was born, my parents began taking me to church. At that time, most churches had services on Sunday morning, Sunday night, and Wednesday night and we were at each one, every week. I had three brothers and no matter how much we complained or gave excuses; we knew where would end up on those days, it might just hurt to sit down more if we complained too much. So you could say that I grew pretty familiar with the routine.

Something changed in that routine one week when I was around five years old. Our pastor painted a vivid picture of the pain and separation from God that would happen to those who do not put their faith in Jesus for the forgiveness of their sins. I still remember that fear and how it brought me to my dad that night. I went to him and asked him if our pastor was telling the truth, and he showed me in the Bible that he was not lying. My dad led me in a simple prayer where I told God I believed that Jesus died for my sins and I asked for God's forgiveness.

I wish I could tell you that I never told another lie, never disobeyed my parents again, but that would be another lie on the list. I do believe that it started me on a journey of change, though. Throughout those formative years, I remember multiple times where I lost my way and started living for myself instead of God. It made me question whether I believed in this Jesus that I gave my life to and whether or not those memories of praying with my father were real. But every time I humbled myself and asked for His forgiveness, God drew me back to Him.

It is my belief that too many people want to point at a date when they prayed a prayer or walked down a church aisle as an assurance that they are all set in their relationship with God. In those times of struggle over the years I had to remind myself that even if my memory fails me and I ca not remember the details or the prayer I prayed, that is not what saves me. As Ephesians 2:8-9 says: **"For by grace you have been saved through faith. And this is not your own doing; it is the gift of God, not a result of works, so that no one may boast."** It is not "do I remember if I prayed a prayer" but "do I believe, TODAY, which Jesus died on the cross and rose again victorious over death to cover my sin? Am I seeing God change me from the inside out? Not that I am perfect or never make mistakes, but can I look back and see the difference He is making in me?"

No matter your personal journey or how long you have been a follower of Jesus, it can become just a routine. Along the way, you will be tempted to leave the path. Don not just point at a date as a golden ticket to Heaven and go off on your way. I hope that you will regularly examine your life and ask God to make your faith living and real.

TESTIMONY 10

BRETT EBERLE
Production Director

For a good portion of my life, I have struggled with people asking me to share my testimony. Who wants to hear a story of some kid who has been in church his whole life? I certainly did not. For years I wondered what it would have been like to have found God on the side of the road when I was at rock bottom, to have had that complete life-altering shift that comes when you first begin to walk with God. It was not until I sat down to write this that I realized that my testimony is amazing, it is the story of how I took my first steps with God.

I have been blessed with many godly role models throughout my life, but my salvation is mainly because of three amazing people. The first comes as a pair, and it may be cliché, but it is my parents. As I sit here and write this, I am almost twenty-four years old, and I have never seen my parents fight. Throughout my life, they have shown me what a godly home and godly life is supposed to look like.

The third person that played a large part in my salvation is a lady by the name of Barb. Growing up both of my parents had full-time jobs, and that meant that my brother and I had to go to a babysitter, Barb was that babysitter. If we are honest, she was way more like a grandma to me than a babysitter. Barb was also my Sunday School teacher, and it was in a small windowless room in the basement of the church that we attended where Barb walked me through the Bible explaining what it meant to have a personal relationship with Jesus.

I am proud of my testimony, and I thank God everyday that I do not know what it means to hit rock bottom. I have stumbled and ran into what felt like brick walls along the way, but nothing can take away the memory of that lady kneeling down at a tiny kids table praying with me and for me.

TESTIMONY 11

WES MCCULLOUGH
Production Director

When I say I have gone to church my whole life, I mean it. When I was born, my parents took me from the hospital straight to church where they prayed over and dedicated me.

Here is my life in a nutshell:

- Both parents are believers and lifetime attendees of church
- I accepted Christ at a very young age and rededicated my life as a teen
- I have attended church nearly every weekend of my life
- I have been serving in the church since I was 14 years-old
- No alcohol, tobacco, drugs, profanity, or sex before marriage

At first glance, my testimony can seem plain, boring, or dull. Hearing a powerful testimony of total life change from sin to salvation can make me think mine is nothing to brag about. A better way to think of my testimony is not salvation OUT of a wicked life but FROM a wicked life completely. I am not claiming to be without sin, but a life of alcohol, drugs, sexual impurity, and lawlessness is one I have never known firsthand. Christian parents raising me with morality and respectfulness, compounded by my shy nature has protected me from making decisions that would send my life spiraling out of control.

God's mercy has allowed me to understand choice and consequence. I have always focused on the negatives that alcohol, drugs, and promiscuity have on one's life. By the grace of God, I have never been tempted by those things. One verse that has always helped is Romans 12:2, ***"Do not be conformed to this world, but be transformed by the renewal of your mind, that by testing you may discern what is the will of God, what is good and acceptable and perfect."*** I have always wanted to be my own person. Be it the partying lifestyle or fashion; I only ever wanted to be me. My duty as a Christian is not to mirror the ways of man but to reflect the image of Christ.

I share my story with humility. I do not think myself better than any other sinner saved by grace. The truth is, hearing of someone who has hit rock bottom and been saved by God is inspiring to someone like me. I hope my testimony is likewise inspiring to them. I want my testimony to be confirmation that God can save you BEFORE you turn the wrong way as well as after. I encourage you to proudly share of God's grace in your life no matter when it happened.

TESTIMONY 12
ERIC JEFFREY
Children's Director

In January of 2002, I made a conscious decision to let Christ take over my life and be my Lord and Savior. This is the testimony of the work the Holy Spirit did before that day.

I grew up in the Catholic Church, I went to Catholic school, I was an altar boy, and my parents were active in the school and the church. I participated in all the sacraments – baptism, communion, first communion, first confession, and confirmation. Let me be clear, I was a willing participant in these activities, but mostly because my parents and the church told me this is what I was supposed to do, so I did.

Going to Catholic school and church, I was taught many things about God, the Holy Spirit, and Jesus; however, it was taught from a catechism book, not the Holy Bible. I never saw a Bible in church or school, we had one at home, but I believe it was hidden, and we never opened it. I remember exactly what it looked like to this day. The thing I took away from the experience with church, looking back, was that if you do this, this, and this you will be forgiven and go to Heaven when it is time. I was never taught salvation through Jesus Christ being the only way to Heaven. In retrospect, though, I believe it was the foundation of a greater work God was going to do.

In eighth grade, my family moved from the city of Detroit to the suburbs of Novi. My parents connected with the local Catholic church, and we continued our weekly visitations to church. As most teens do, I became self-aware that I am my own person and began to question all authority – parental, educational, and spiritual. At some point, I do not remember exactly when my parents informed me that when I turn 16 that it would be my responsibility to get to church since I could drive and hold down a job. So when I hit the age of accountability, I stopped going to church except on Christmas and Easter. This was only to appease my parents.

After that, I soon began to explore drugs and alcohol and began a serious relationship with both. For many years I abused all kinds of drugs and decided alcohol was not my thing. My drug use was habitual and constant. I did it responsibly (sounds weird) by going to school and holding down various jobs to support my habit. Later on, I married, and even sooner I was divorced because I wanted my relationship with drugs more than anything. The ink on the divorce papers was not even dry before I was abusing more than ever. All the while I can remember thinking about God from time to time and thinking, "I am a good person, I have not killed anyone, plus I am Catholic."

Then I began a relationship with my current wife, Diane, of 17 years. I am not sure what she saw in me but, we became an item. I continued my drug use; then I had some sort of revelation. This lifestyle is getting me nowhere. With the encouragement of Diane (wife now), I quit drugs. I began to pursue higher education, landed a new career, and boom I was on my way. One thing, though, I still did not feel right in some unexplainable way. We moved onto a lake and built a house together and got married in it. The accomplishment of building your house was a great experience, but still, something was missing.

After we had settled into the new house, a man that lived kitty corner from us came over and introduced himself. He would be the man that would lead me to Christ. His name was Jack Russell. This was soon after the events of September 11, 2001. He began to witness to me regularly, and I would say to him, "I am good. I am Catholic. I got it covered." We played floor hockey together so he would drive us to and from and use it as an opportunity witness and invite me to his church. I spoke to my wife about going, and she was in agreement, so we went to Faith Baptist Church. I went and enjoyed the speaking of the pastor (Pastor Jim). Soon after we joined a Bible study seven steps to joy, taught by Jack because I felt the need to learn the Bible, not religion. After about the second or third lesson, I felt so lost. I was just not getting it. I was reading the lessons and doing the questions, but I just did not get it. I wanted to, but it seemed like I could not grasp it. Jack shared some Scriptures with me. 1 Corinthians 2:14, Ephesians 2:8-9, and the power of God's Holy Word began to penetrate my spirit and changed me from the inside out. Jack continued relentlessly to pound me with God's Word full of truth and love. On January 13, 2002, I bent my knee on the steps in the auditorium at Faith Baptist Church and asked Christ to enter my life and thankfully I was never the same. The odd thing about that day was that I told Jack during the week that I would come to church Sunday and make a profession of faith. In my mind, I was thinking, "I will have to do this (profess Christ) just to get this guy off my back about Jesus." The Lord truly works in mysterious ways.

Today I have the privilege of teaching kids the Word of God at the same church where I gave my life to Christ. I am thankful for the people God placed in my life that encouraged me to make a decision to follow Christ. This is the testimony of Jesus Christ's work in the life of this man, Eric M Jeffrey.

growing is messy
is hard
is labor intensive

18

GROWING IN THE WORD

"*Teaching them to observe all that I have commanded you. And behold, I am with you always, to the end of the age*" (glorify God by growing in the Word).

"There is no growth without change, no change without fear or loss and no loss without pain." Rick Warren

What does this quote mean? _____
_____ Its scary (fear) _____
_____
_____

How does it relate to spiritual growth? _____
_____
_____
_____

2 Timothy 3:16-17
"*All Scripture is breathed out by God and profitable for teaching, for reproof, for correction, and for training in righteousness, that the man of God may be complete, equipped for every good work.*"

What thoughts come to mind when you read "breathed out by God"? _____
_____
_____

In your own words, how is the Bible useful? _____
_____
_____
_____

2 Timothy 2:15
"Do your best to present yourself to God as one approved, a worker who has no need to be ashamed, rightly handling the word of truth."

What steps should be taken to have a better handle on the Bible?
1. Read it — John first
pray —   — commit to memory
meditate —

Proverbs 27:17
"Iron sharpens iron, and one man sharpens another."

This is a man's man verse (I think the Hebrew might even imply some grunting). What does it mean for men? _____
_____
Same - thing -
Men -
What does it mean for women? _____
_____
_____
_____

Accountability —
Challenge
Speak truths

When my son was in first grade, he asked me, "Dad, why don't we go straight to Heaven when we get saved?" His question caught me, impressed me, challenged me, and has stuck with me. I answered that if people immediately went to Heaven, who would have told us about Jesus?

What answer would you give? _____
_____
_____

The emphasis of GROW is not for self alone, but to GO and make a difference in the world. This is why we need to Reach, Gather, Grow, and back to Reach.

Who should your growth community reach out to? _____
_____
_____
_____

Who should you personally reach out to? _____
_____
_____
_____

Romans 1:16
"For I am not ashamed of the gospel, for it is the power of God for salvation to everyone who believes, to the Jew first and also to the Greek."

"To be a Christian without prayer is no more possible than to be alive without breathing." Martin Luther

How is prayer valuable? _____
_____
_____
_____

What other Christian disciplines are vital? _____
_____
_____
_____

TESTIMONY 13

RANDY "DOC" JOHNSON
Growth Pastor

My story begins before I was born. My parents were not raised in Christian homes. My mom and her sister were "bus kids." Her parents did not take them to church but allowed them to attend on their own. They both heard the Good News of Jesus Christ and gave their lives to Him. My dad became a follower of Jesus Christ in his late teens when he attended a Billy Graham crusade and heard the Gospel. A bus driver and Billy Graham are equally important in my story.

Even though my parents were not raised in a Christian home, they figured it out. I was raised in a loving, Christ-honoring home. We went to First Baptist Church of Hazel Park for Sunday School, the Sunday morning service, the Sunday evening service, Wednesday night prayer meeting, and as I grew older all camps and youth events. It did not feel forced or awkward. It was what we did. We even had family devotions and prayer each morning before school.

There is an important side note to my story. My aunt who was a "bus kid" with my mom, married a Christian man. Their mom, my grandmother, later became a follower of Christ. They were all very close. So my mom and dad built a house right across the street from my grandmother, and my aunt and uncle built right next to them. We had our Christian community just south of 9 Mile.

At age seven, just after morning family devotions, I prayed "asking Jesus into my heart." I was not baptized until I was twelve. My parents wanted to make sure I understood that baptism did not save me and that it was to be a stepping up point telling others of my desire to follow Jesus. When I was in high school, our church hired a new Youth Pastor, Dave Hulbert. Pastor Dave, or Radar as we called him, became a dear friend for me. We spent a lot of time together. It was at this point I realized God was calling me to be a Pastor.

I hear people say they had a "drug" problem – they were "drug" to every Church event and became bitter. I did not experience that. I am thankful for my parents and my Church family. I even met Angela at church. We were high school sweethearts from Youth Group. It does not get much better than that.

A verse that has challenged and encouraged me is 1 Thessalonians 5:11, **"Therefore encourage one another and build one another up, just as you are doing."** I hope my story will help you to daily choose to follow Jesus for yourself and your family.

TESTIMONY 14

JAYSON COMBS
Family Pastor

Man, did I ever hate life. It was the first day of my freshmen year of high school. I walked into a brand new school, not knowing a single soul. That summer, I had moved from the suburbs of Detroit to what felt like the suburbs of nothing. My dad had recently retired from General Motors and became the Pastor of a very small church on the corner of a corn field. We moved from everything we knew, including friends, family, and our home church, to the small farming community of Pigeon, Michigan. The town had one stop and no fast food restaurants. The closest mall was an hour away, and my friends were two hours away. I just wanted to go back home, to all my friends and quite frankly...civilization. Man, did I ever hate my life.

For many weeks, I spent a lot of time alone. Most evenings, I would go into my basement, flip the ping pong table up and hit the ball back and forth to myself...over and over and over again. I got pretty good. Yet, it was easy for me to sit in my loneliness and ask why? Why here, God? Even though God felt a million miles away, He was still in control, and things slowly began to change.

A few weeks into that school year, I found a group of kids that seemed pretty cool. Some of them went to a small Mennonite church, and they invited me to their church Bible study. Very quickly, I realized these kids had a sincere faith. It was not too long after that that we started to have our own Thursday night small group. Because we all went to small churches and none of us had an official youth pastor, we decided to lead our own Bible studies and alternate homes each week. We began to invite people from school and would sometimes have over forty high school students on any given night. We would take turns talking about what God was teaching us throughout the week and challenged each other to dig deeper into God's Word for understanding. We were doing small groups before small groups were even cool.

The church my dad pastored was very small. The youth group consisted of me...and me. But during my sophomore year of high school, we started a kid's club ministry held on Wednesday nights. The church was able to purchase a 15 passenger van to pick up kids from two neighboring towns. As a 16-year old, I would drive to one town to pick up as many as 25 kids. Yes, I know I was 16, and yes, the van was packed. I think the statute of limitations is up, however, so I think I am okay. Anyway, I would drop the kids off at church before driving to the next town for another 25 or so kids. My mom did the crafts and music each week, but I taught the Bible lesson before driving the kids home. Kid's club on Wednesday nights is where I ultimately learned to teach the Word, love kids, and serve. God blessed that ministry, and a seed was planted in my heart to minister to God's people.

As I reflect on those years in high school, I now see that it was a defining moment in my life. I had grown up in the church, and I was saved at a young age, but God took those four years and discipled me into a true follower of Jesus. Man, I am so thankful for that time in my life.

TESTIMONY 15

LAURA COMBS
Wife of Pastor Jayson Combs

The moment we accept Christ as Lord and Savior, we have a calling on our lives to follow and serve Christ as our Lord and to walk in His ways. I believe, however, God was working in my life, personally, for generations. My grandmother, a God-fearing woman with "unfeigned [genuine] faith" as described in Paul's second letter to Timothy, along with my grandfather, passed on a spiritual heritage more important than money can buy. But it did not start with her. Grandma recalled her own father, my great-grandfather, living out the words from Deuteronomy 6:4-7,

"Hear, O Israel: The Lord our God, the Lord is one. You shall love the Lord your God with all your heart and with all your soul and with all your might. And these words that I command you today shall be on your heart. You shall teach them diligently to your children, and shall talk of them when you sit in your house, and when you walk by the way, and when you lie down, and when you rise."

From as young as I can remember, I was told my great-grandfather took the words from Deuteronomy to heart and prayed the following words often during bedtime devotion and prayer, "Lord, I pray for the salvation of each of my children, and their children, and their children's children, and their children's children's children. Amen." Now, if I get my "children's children" correct, my great-grandfather prayed directly for the salvation of my mother, for me, and even for my son! Wow! How amazing! And not only did he pray for our salvation alone, but he diligently taught the Word to his own children and further passed on an importance of loving the Lord, loving His Word, and walking in His Word each and every day. I am forever grateful for the legacy of my great-grandfather, my grandmother, and my mother.

Of course, it has not always been easy. There have been significant moments and trials in my life where I had to decide for myself whether I would follow the Lord, or just ride on my families' coattails. God's faithfulness, however, has undoubtedly been evident. The testimonies and stories in my immediate and extended family of God's faithfulness are simply undeniable! Their stories are His Story, and I only desire for my story to reflect His Story as well.

Consequently, I am compelled and persuaded to pray the same prayer my great-grandfather prayed. Lord, I pray for the salvation of my children, and of their children, and their children's children, and their children's children's children. And further, I pray they will fall in love with God and fall in love with God's Word. Our own flesh, the world, and the enemy will seek to destroy us. Only our faith in God and feasting on His Word will guide and direct us along the path of life. What heritage will you pass on? Do you love God's Word? Do you want the generations after you, and even the people around you, to love God and His Word? How will you show them? What will you do?

As my grandmother also prayed, "God grant that the circle will be unbroken." Pass on a Christian heritage that will never by broken!

TESTIMONY 16

CHRIS CAIN
Women's Ministry Director

The year was 1995, and I was invited to go to church. I had been awaiting an invite. I wanted my kids in church. You see, I had been doing all of the "right" things; reading them Bible stories, praying with them, even enrolling them in a preschool that was held inside a church building. So, now I just had to get them to church to be baptized, and that would be it, they would be set. Right? Kind of funny how I thought it would be good for them to be in church, but not necessary for me. It was not necessary because there was no hope for me.

I was raised in a home where we went to church every Sunday. My loving parents worked hard and had solid values. Summers were filled with VBS, and for most of my childhood a Gingellville Baptist Church bus picked me up for AWANA every Monday night. I was a good kid. But then, in 1983, at age 17, I did something that would change my world. I messed up. And I was going straight to hell. The guilt and shame that would follow me for over a decade were overwhelming. I hated myself. I deserved hell. There were people along the way who tried to help me. They would say, "Oh you just need to learn to forgive yourself" or "Time will heal all things" or "Do not be so hard on yourself."

The day arrived. I managed to get myself and four kids ages three months to five years old, fed, dressed, and ready on time. That sweet church in Waterford was so welcoming to us. They were so helpful. I even signed up to be on the ladies' softball team. Wow, this was exactly what I wanted for my children. They loved it. I loved it. Week after week we went Sunday mornings, Sunday nights, midweek services, any time that the doors were open. This was home.

As I began to fall in love with the Word and with Jesus, I began to see that there really might be some hope for me. Those Scriptures I had memorized as a child in AWANA started to come alive. The love and grace of Jesus were so powerful, but I still could not seem to transfer what I knew of Him and His Word into my own past circumstances and life. Again, I heard from others, "You need to forgive yourself" or "Time heals all wounds." That did not make sense to me. But it did drive me deeper into the Word. And somewhere between Genesis 1:1 and Revelation 22:21 I saw that God's promises stand. I saw the ways He brings His promises to fulfillment and my trust in His faithfulness grew. I can stand on those promises, even when I do not understand the circumstances that seem to contradict it. No, I did not need to forgive myself, I just had to trust in His proven faithfulness. I was determined that I was no longer going to allow my past to become greater than what Jesus did for me. I did not need time. I needed The Healer! He forgave me; He delivered me, He loves me, then and now.

TESTIMONY 17

HOLLY WELLS
Assistant to the Pastor

Pastor Jim has talked about "John 3" and "John 4" believers – essentially those who grew up in the Church and those who did not. Well, I am a part of the John 4 group; I did not grow up in a Christian home or Church. I did, however, spend a couple of years during my early childhood in Catholic private school. I was about 8 or 9 years old at the time and do not remember much other than panicking over the prayers I was supposed to recite to some scary priest during confession to make my first communion. My mom, older sister, and I were CEO Catholics (attending Christmas, Easter, and Other) while my dad was apparently an atheist at the time.

Fast forward a few years, my parents were now divorced, and life was a gigantic mess. My dad was living with his new family while my older sister, a young teenager, fought with my mom constantly, and I became my mom's confidant as she shared the pain of divorce and worries of being a single mom. And my life soon became rooted in fear. I feared that my sister would carry out threats she made against my mom in anger and hurt. I feared that my mom would follow through when she told me she wanted to drive off a mountain near where we lived. And I eventually shut down emotionally when my dad stopped talking to me for over a year when I did not stay the night with him and his new family at Christmas. I experienced immense brokenness for the first time in my life, and all I knew to do was to "be good" because everything else was so bad. So much happened during these next several years including an abusive dating relationship where fear ran deeper and grew higher than ever before. I internalized all of it while coming to my own conclusions that "this is just how relationships are" ...that is until someone told me the truth: this <u>was not</u> how relationships were supposed to be.

This person and I were dating by this point, and four years later, he and I were married. In our early 20s, we were trying to figure out life and marriage while working and going to school. Life was good – we were best friends and had the best time together. We had decent jobs, a house, cars – nothing extravagant but nice. We "checked-in" to church most Sundays to only "check-out" as soon as service ended. We were benchwarmers for about one and a half hours on Sundays as "Christians," then back into the world, we went! It is no surprise that without the Lord, our marriage was a ticking time bomb. As the years set in, so did life. The newness of being newlyweds wore off, selfishness became priority, and soon our own agendas became more important than the other person. Sin is sin no matter how you slice and dice it – and sin kills.

We made it about six years before we were separated and living apart with very hardened hearts, fighting constantly and without much regard toward one another or to God. I was already receiving biblically-based counseling to work through my past and continued with it, slowly learning about God. My counselor recommended DivorceCare, so I started attending every week. I learned more about God's Word, His character, and heart as well as His truth and instruction about the marriage covenant and divorce. A few months went by, and my heart began to change.

As I learned about God's presence, faithfulness, redemption, safety, and love for me, He gently and patiently waited for me to trust Him. The Lord used Psalm 139 to minister to my heart, and I became His. Verse 14 says, **"I will praise You, for I am fearfully and wonderfully made, Marvelous are Your works, And that my soul knows very well"** (NKJV). God continued to meet me in all of my brokenness, in all of my pain, in all of my shame and sins. He started making changes in my life, and by the Holy Spirit inside of me; He led me to pursue reconciliation with my husband on several occasions. I knew and believed with great conviction and without any hesitation that God desired to redeem our marriage. I knew He could do it; I prayed for years that He would. It did not matter to me that our divorce became final, I still believed He could do it. The thing is, while God does desire to restore and heal marriages for our good and His glory, His priority is our individual relationship with Him one-on-one.

It has been over ten years since giving my life back to the Lord, and in this short amount of time, He has done an incredible work. He has been ever so faithful to me each moment of every day. God, my Father, has been with me through all the tears and healing processes of life (and forever will be).

As I seek Him, He continues to teach me more about Himself as my Redeemer, Provider, Protector, Counselor, Best Friend, and more.

TESTIMONY 18

JAMES CLOUSE
Student Pastor

Growing up at Faith Church was a blessing that is beyond what words can describe. Being raised a Catholic I truly never understood what salvation meant until I attended a church camp with Faith when I was 12 years old. It was the Summer of 1995 that I surrendered my life to Jesus Christ.

From the time of 1995 to my high school years, there were many people from Faith Church who had an impact on my life including youth pastors, student leaders, and Pastor Jim. These people helped mold me into the man, the husband, the father, and the pastor that I am today. Without them, I do not believe I would be where I am at today.

In high school, on a church missions trip to Mexico, I felt a tug on my heart to ministry of some sorts. At the time I did not know how that looked. The years went by, and I felt that God had something special planned for my life.

Finally, I listened to God and His plan for my life and knew that I belonged in full-time ministry. There were many amongst the church that pushed me to pursue an education, and I kept pushing that aside. My wife Amanda and I were working with the youth group at the Waterford campus, and I knew that was where I belonged...with teenagers. I finally started pursuing what it took to become a Youth Minister. A couple of years later I graduated from Liberty University and started searching for a job. I knew that it would be only God that could uproot me from Faith.

He did just that. God moved my family to Georgia to be a Student Pastor. It was one of the hardest things I have ever had to do;

to move away from my church and my family. But I knew that God had a plan for us. While in Georgia, God taught me so much about ministry and how to be a Pastor. He taught me how to have a deeper appreciation for who He is and how He works in our lives, how to have a closer relationship with Him and how to be an effective Pastor.

Three and a half years later I received a call from The River Goodrich to be their new Student Pastor. This was a dream come true; to work for the man that I admired so much growing up. Now I know that God has so much in store for me here and I can not wait to work together to show the surrounding communities the light of Christ.

OUR MISSION

Matthew 28:19-20: *"Go therefore and make disciples of all nations, baptizing them in the name of the Father and of the Son and of the Holy Spirit, teaching them to observe all that I have commanded you. And behold, I am with you always, to the end of the age."*

REACH

At The River Church, you will often hear the phrase, "we don't go to church, we are the Church." We believe that as God's people, our primary purpose and goal is to go out and make disciples of Jesus Christ. We encourage you to reach the world in your local communities.

GATHER

Weekend Gatherings at The River Church are all about Jesus, through singing, giving, serving, baptizing, taking the Lord's Supper, and participating in messages that are all about Jesus and bringing glory to Him. We know that when followers of Christ gather together in unity, it's not only a refresher it's bringing life-change.

GROW

Our Growth Communities are designed to mirror the early church in Acts as having "all things in common." They are smaller collections of believers who spend time together studying the word, knowing and caring for one another relationally, and learning to increase their commitment to Christ by holding one another accountable.

The River Church
8393 E. Holly Rd. Holly, MI 48442
theriverchurch.cc • info@theriverchurch.cc

BOOKS BY THE RIVER CHURCH

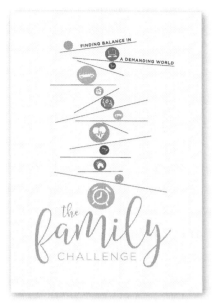
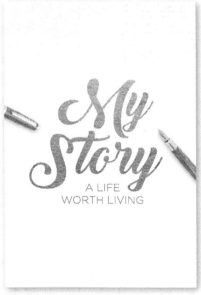
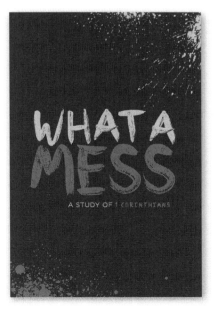

Made in the USA
Lexington, KY
22 May 2017